ECDL®

European Computer Driving Licence®

ECDL Spreadsheets
BCS ITQ L2 Spreadsheet Software

Using Microsoft® Excel® 2016

Syllabus Version 5.0

This training, which has been approved by BCS, The Chartered Institute for IT, includes exercise items intended to assist learners in their training for an ECDL Certification Programme. These exercises are not ECDL certification tests. For information about Approved Centres in the UK please visit the BCS website at www.bcs.org/ecdl.

Release ECDL308_UKv1

Published by: CiA Training Ltd
                   Business & Innovation Centre
                   Sunderland Enterprise Park
                   Sunderland
                   SR5 2TA
                   United Kingdom

                   Tel: +44 (0) 191 549 5002
                   Fax: +44 (0) 191 549 9005

                   E-mail: info@ciatraining.co.uk
                   Web: www.ciatraining.co.uk

ISBN: 978-0-85741-191-4

This guide was written for *Microsoft Office 2016* running on *Windows*. If using a different version of *Office* some features and dialog boxes may not look and function exactly as described.

Office 2016 is optimised to work with touch-screen controls and online file storage. However, this guide assumes you are using a traditional mouse and keyboard and save your files locally.

A screen resolution of *1024x768* is also assumed. Working at a different resolution (or with an application window which is not maximised) may change the look of the dynamic *Office 2016 Ribbon*. For example, if space is restricted, a group of buttons may be replaced by a single button which, when clicked, will display the full group.

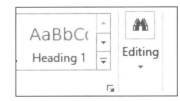

First published 2016.

This courseware may be used to assist learners to prepare for the ECDL Certification Programme as titled on the courseware. Neither BCS nor **CiA Training Ltd** warrants that the use of this courseware publication will ensure passing of the tests for that ECDL Certification Programme.

This courseware publication has been independently reviewed and approved by BCS as covering the learning objectives for the ECDL Certification Programme.

Confirmation of this approval can be obtained by reviewing www.bcs.org/ecdl.

The material contained in this courseware publication has not been reviewed for technical accuracy and does not guarantee that candidates will pass the test for the ECDL Certification Programme.

Any and all assessment items and/or performance-based exercises contained in this courseware relate solely to this publication and do not constitute or imply certification by BCS or ECDL Foundation in respect of the ECDL Certification Programme or any other ECDL test.

Irrespective of how the material contained in this courseware is deployed, for example in a learning management system (LMS) or a customised interface, nothing should suggest to the candidate that this material constitutes certification or can lead to certification through any other process than official ECDL certification testing.

For details on sitting a test for an ECDL certification programme in the UK, please visit the BCS website at www.bcs.org/ecdl.

Learners using this courseware must be registered with BCS before undertaking a test for ECDL. Without a valid registration, the test(s) cannot be undertaken and no certificate, nor any other form of recognition, can be given to a learner. Registration should be undertaken with BCS at an Approved Centre.

Downloading the Data Files

Data files accompanying this guide allow you to learn and practise new skills without the need for lots of data entry. These files must be downloaded from the Internet. Go to **www.ciatraining.co.uk/data** and follow the simple on-screen instructions.

Your *FastCode* for this guide's data is: **ECDL308**

The data files should be installed in the following location on your computer:

Documents \ DATA FILES \ ECDL \ Spreadsheet Software

Aims

The aim of this guide is to familiarise you with the main operating features of *Microsoft Excel* and to provide an understanding of fundamental spreadsheet concepts. This includes practical experience in the design and implementation of basic spreadsheets.

Objectives

After completing the guide you will be able to:

- Work with spreadsheets and save them in different file formats

- Enter data into cells and use good practice in creating lists; select, sort, copy, move and delete data

- Edit rows and columns in a worksheet; copy, move, delete and appropriately rename worksheets

- Create mathematical and logical formulas using standard spreadsheet functions; use good practice in formula creation and be able to recognise error values in formulas

- Format numbers and text content in a spreadsheet

- Choose, create and format charts to communicate information meaningfully

- Adjust spreadsheet page settings and check and correct spreadsheet content before finally printing spreadsheets.

Assessment of Knowledge

At the end of this guide is a **Record of Achievement Matrix**. Before the guide is started, it is recommended that you complete the matrix to measure your current level of knowledge. After working through a section, return to and update the **Record of Achievement**. Only when you feel you are competent in all areas should you move on to the next section.

Contents

Section 1
Getting Started

By the end of this section you should be able to:

Understand Spreadsheet Principles

Start a Spreadsheet Program

Recognise the Spreadsheet Screen Layout

Use the Ribbon and Quick Access Toolbar

Use Help

Change Preferences

Close a Spreadsheet Program

Work through the **Driving Lessons** in this section to gain an understanding of the above features.

For each **Driving Lesson**, read all of the **Park and Read** instructions and then perform the numbered steps of the **Manoeuvres**. Complete the **Revision** exercise(s) at the end of the section to test your knowledge.

Driving Lesson 1 - Starting Excel

 Park and Read

Excel is an extremely useful Spreadsheet application (or "app") created specifically to help in the processing of tabular information, usually numbers. The spreadsheet stores information in rows (across the screen) and columns (down the screen), forming a worksheet (the *Excel* term for a spreadsheet).

Spreadsheets are most commonly used to manipulate figures. They can be used for accounting, cash flows, budgeting, forecasts, etc. Any job that involves the use of numbers can be done on a spreadsheet.

The biggest advantage that a spreadsheet has over other methods of manipulating data is its ability to constantly update figures without the user having to do any calculations. Once a spreadsheet is set up, its calculations will always be correct and any changes in data are automatically updated.

Spreadsheets can also take raw data and present it in an attractive way, with formatted tables and charts.

 *The steps required to start* Excel *vary slightly depending on the version of Windows installed on your computer.*

 Manoeuvres

1.   Start your computer and log in to *Windows*.

2.   Find and click the **Start** button, or ⊞, found towards the bottom left corner of the **Desktop** on the **Taskbar**.

3.   The **Start Menu** appears. Click **All Programs** or **All apps** at the bottom of the **Start Menu** to show a list of available programs.

 *If you are using* Windows 8, *a full* **Start Screen** *may be shown instead.* **All Programs** *will appear as a downwards facing arrow.*

4.   Find and click the entry for the spreadsheet program **Excel 2016**. You may need to scroll to find it.

 You can also type **Excel** *when the* **Start Menu** *is open to search for and start the program. You may also find a button for it on the* **Taskbar**.

5.   *Excel* starts and appears in its own window. Leave the application open for the next lesson.

Driving Lesson 2 - The Excel Screen

🅿 Park and Read

When first started, *Excel* displays a welcome screen showing a selection of templates that can be used to create new spreadsheets. Any recently opened files will be listed on the left.

↱ Manoeuvres

1. Examine the *Excel* welcome screen. Notice the list of templates that can be used to create new spreadsheets.

2. Click **Blank workbook**. *Excel* displays a new, blank workbook named **Book1** (as shown in the **Title Bar**). A **workbook** is a file that can contain many **worksheets**.

3. The *Excel* screen will be similar to the screenshot below. Check the captions and identify the parts on the screen. **Sheet1** is displayed.

4. The **Title Bar** is the top line of the *Excel* screen. It shows the application and the name of the workbook that is on the screen. Identify the **Title Bar**.

5. The name of the current workbook is **Book1** or similar. Check this in the **Title Bar**.

Driving Lesson 2 - Continued

6. At the top left of the screen the first tab on the **Ribbon** is the **File** tab, . This displays a list of basic program functions such as; **Open**, **Save**, **Print** and **Close**.

7. Immediately above this button is the **Quick Access Toolbar**.

8. By default this contains three main buttons, **Save**, **Undo** and **Redo**. More buttons can be added.

9. Under the **Quick Access Toolbar** is an area called the **Ribbon**. This consists of a range of tabs containing buttons within groups (which you will learn more about in the next lesson).

10. The buttons are used to select an action or basic feature. Move the cursor over any button but do not click. Read the **ToolTip** that appears which gives the name of that button and a small description, e.g. **Italic** in the **Font** group.

11. The **Status Bar** runs along the bottom of the window. This displays messages as tasks are performed. Check that the current message, at the left, states **Ready**.

12. The right side of the **Status Bar** contains **View** buttons and a **Zoom** slider.

13. Leave the application open for the next lesson.

Driving Lesson 3 - The Ribbon

▣ Park and Read

Excel 2016 has a **Ribbon** which is displayed at the top of the application window. The **Ribbon** contains buttons and drop-down lists to control the operation of *Excel*. The **Ribbon** is divided into a series of **Tabs**, each one of which has a set of controls specific to a certain function or process. On each tab, the controls are further divided into separate **Groups** of connected functions.

Some tabs can be selected manually, whereas some only appear when certain operations are active (for example, only when a **Chart** is active will three **CHART TOOLS** tabs be displayed).

⟳ Manoeuvres

1. On the **Ribbon**, the **Home** tab should currently be selected. Other basic tabs are available.

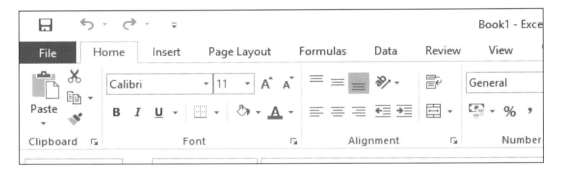

*Part of the **Ribbon** displaying the **Home** tab*

ⓘ *Any buttons displayed in pale grey are called ghosted and are not available to be selected at present.*

2. Notice how the buttons on the **Ribbon** are divided into **Groups** (**Clipboard**, **Font**, **Alignment**, etc.).

ⓘ *The display of buttons on the **Ribbon** is dynamic. That is, it will change according to how much space there is available. If the window is not maximised or the screen resolution is anything other than 1024 x 768, the **Ribbon** will not always appear exactly as shown in this guide.*

3. Some buttons produce immediate effects like the **Bold**, **Italic** and **Underline** buttons in the **Font** group.

4. Buttons with a drop-down arrow lead to further options. Click the **Find & Select** button which is available in the **Editing** group. A list of further options is displayed.

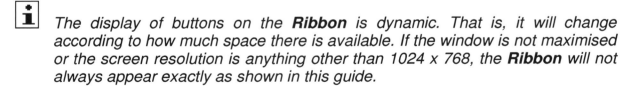

Driving Lesson 3 - Continued

5. Some options will display a dialog box which needs data to be entered. Click the first option, **Find**, and the **Find and Replace** dialog box is displayed.

6. Click the **Close** button on the dialog box to remove it.

7. Some groups have a dialog box launcher button, ⌐◣, to the right of the group name, e.g. the **Font** group, Font ⌐◣.

8. Click the **Font** dialog box launcher to display the **Format Cells** dialog box.

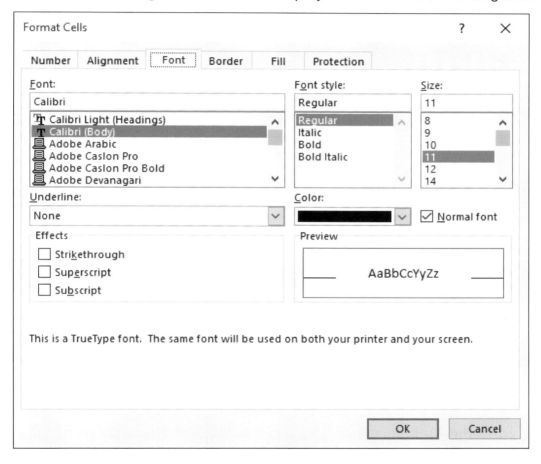

9. This is a tabbed dialog box; each tab at the top (e.g. **Number**, **Alignment**, **Font**) can be clicked to see a different set of options. Try it. When you are finished, click **Cancel** to close the dialog box.

10. Display the other basic tabs one at a time: **Insert**, **Page Layout**, **Formulas, Data**, **Review** and **View** to see which other commands are available.

ℹ️ *There may be a **DEVELOPER** tab displayed, used for controlling macros. This tab is usually not displayed by default.*

11. Select the **Home** tab again.

Driving Lesson 4 - Quick Access Toolbar

▣ Park and Read

Most commands in *Excel* are accessed via the **Ribbon**. Above the **Ribbon** is the **Quick Access Toolbar** which contains a few popular command buttons. By default this toolbar has three buttons: **Save**, **Undo** and **Redo**. This toolbar can be customised by adding further buttons.

⤵ Manoeuvres

1. Locate the **Quick Access Toolbar** at the top left corner of the window.

2. Point at each button and read its **ToolTip**. There have been no actions performed yet, so the last two buttons are ghosted (but they still have ToolTips).

3. To the right of the buttons is the **Customize Quick Access Toolbar** button, ⟨▾⟩. Click the button to display a menu. You can add any of the buttons shown by simply clicking them.

4. To add commands not shown, select **More Commands**. This displays **Excel Options**, which is covered later in this guide. For now, click **Cancel** to close **Excel Options**.

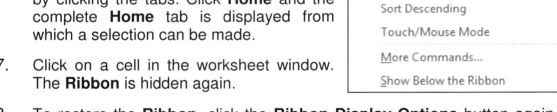

5. Minimize the **Ribbon** by clicking the **Ribbon Display Options** button, ⟨⬆⟩, which is located at the top right of the screen. Select the **Show Tabs** option.

6. The **Ribbon** is hidden with only the tabs displayed. The ribbon is accessed again by clicking the tabs. Click **Home** and the complete **Home** tab is displayed from which a selection can be made.

7. Click on a cell in the worksheet window. The **Ribbon** is hidden again.

8. To restore the **Ribbon**, click the **Ribbon Display Options** button again, ⟨⬆⟩ and select **Show Tabs and Commands**. The **Ribbon** is displayed normally again.

ℹ️ *The **Ribbon** can also be minimized by right clicking on it and selecting the* ***Collapse the Ribbon*** *option. To restore the **Ribbon** right click on any tab and uncheck **Collapse the Ribbon**. There is also a **Collapse the Ribbon** button at the right end of the **Ribbon**, ⟨˄⟩.*

Driving Lesson 5 - The Worksheet Window

▣ Park and Read

Spreadsheets help in the processing of numbers. They store information arranged in **rows** (across the screen) and **columns** (down the screen). A **cell** is the intersection of a row and column. It is good practice for each filled cell to contain only a single element of data.

All the cells form a **worksheet** (the *Excel* term for a spreadsheet). Several **worksheets** are bound together and called a **workbook**.

⮌ Manoeuvres

1. Each cell is identified by a column letter and row number which form an intersection, e.g. the cell formed where column **D** and row **8** meet is known as cell **D8**. Move the mouse pointer to cell **B3** and click. The **Current** or **Active** cell is now **B3**. It has a dark green border.

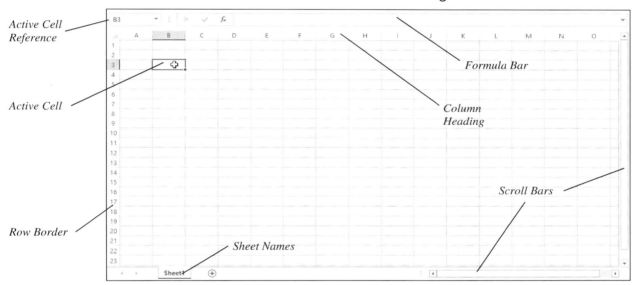

2. Look for the **Active Cell Reference,** which is shown in the **Name Box** at the left of the **Formula Bar**. It displays **B3**.

3. Click in cell **C6**. The **Active Cell Reference** now shows **C6**. These letters and numbers are shown highlighted in the **Row** and **Column Headings** on the worksheet. **C6** is now the **Current** or **Active cell**.

4. The active cell can be moved using various key presses. Press the right cursor key →. The active cell moves right into cell **D6**.

5. Press the down cursor ↓ to move into cell **D7**. Press the left cursor ← to move into **C7**.

6. Press the up cursor ↑ . The active cell should now be **C6** again.

Driving Lesson 6 - Moving Around

▣ Park and Read

A worksheet is very large. The arrow keys are used for moving small distances. Other keys are used to move bigger distances.

☞ Manoeuvres

1. Use the right cursor key → repeatedly to move to the column after **Z**. The alphabet is used again with **A** in front, i.e. **AA AB ...**, then **BA, BB ...**, etc.

2. The <**End**> key followed by an arrow key moves to the edge of the worksheet when empty. To move to the last column press <**End**> then the right arrow key →. The last column is **XFD** (column 16384).

3. Press the <**Home**> key. This always returns the active cell to column **A** on the same row.

4. Click on cell **D3**. Press <**End**> followed by the → key to move to **XFD3**.

5. Press the <**Home**> key to return to cell **A3**.

6. Press <**End**> then the **Down** cursor key ↓. The active cell moves down to the last row, **1048576**.

7. Press <**Ctrl Home**> (hold down the **Control** key and press the **Home** key) to move back to cell **A1**. The key press <**Ctrl Home**> always moves the active cell back to **A1**.

8. Click on a cell in the centre of the screen and press <**Ctrl Home**> to move to **A1** again.

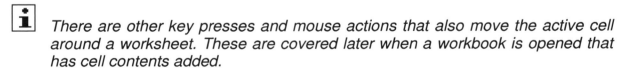

There are other key presses and mouse actions that also move the active cell around a worksheet. These are covered later when a workbook is opened that has cell contents added.

Driving Lesson 7 - Help

▣ Park and Read

Excel 2016 features a new task-based **Help** facility. To use it you simply tell *Excel* what it is you are trying to do – it will then find help online or even perform the task for you.

⤴ Manoeuvres

1. Locate the new **Tell Me** box on the **Ribbon**. You can find this to the right of the **View** tab.

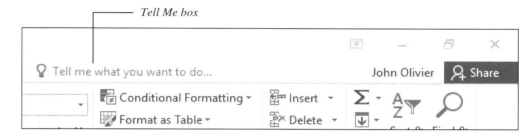

Tell Me box

2. You can use the **Tell Me** box to find help on a specific task. Let's try it…

3. Assume you would like to insert a picture in the current worksheet. Click once on the **Tell Me** box and type **Insert a picture** (don't press <**Enter**>).

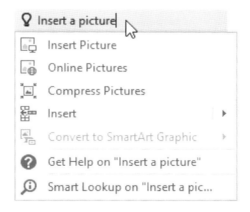

4. A number of command suggestions appear (features that *Excel* recommends using to achieve your task). For now, click **Get Help on "Insert a picture"** to search the web for help.

5. An **Excel 2016 Help** window appears with a number of help topics listed. Scan the topics shown and click the one that looks the most relevant.

ℹ️ *You can use this technique to find help on any* Excel *questions you have. Topics can also be printed for reference by clicking the **Print** button,* 🖨.

6. Click the **Back** button, ⬅, to move back to the previous screen. You can now follow another link.

Driving Lesson 7 - Continued

7. When you are finished exploring the online help system, close the **Excel 2016 Help** window by clicking its **Close** button, ✕ .

 *You can also display the **Excel 2016 Help** window by displaying the **File** tab and clicking **Microsoft Excel Help**, ?, on the **Title Bar** (or by pressing <F1>).*

8. Click the **Tell Me** box and type **Insert a picture** again. This time, select the suggested command **Insert Picture**.

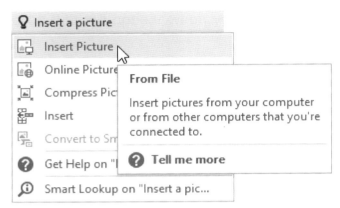

 *Clicking a suggested command in the **Tell Me** box is the same as finding and clicking its button on the **Ribbon**. In this case, clicking **Insert Picture** in the **Tell Me** box is the same as displaying the **Insert** tab and clicking the **Pictures** button in the **Illustrations** group.*

9. The **Insert Picture** dialog box appears. You will learn more about this feature later, so for now click **Cancel**.

10. Let's try another. Type **Zoom** in the **Tell Me** box and select the first suggested command, **Zoom**.

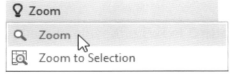

 *Clicking **Zoom** in the **Tell Me** box is the same as displaying the **View** tab and clicking the **Zoom** button in the **Zoom** group.*

11. The **Zoom** dialog box appears which allows you to adjust zoom levels. Again, you will learn more about zooming later, so for now click **Cancel**.

12. Next, try entering **Make text bold** into the **Tell Me** box. This time, press <**Enter**> to accept the first suggested command (**Bold**) and notice the **Bold** button is activated on the **Home** tab. Any text entered in the current selected cell will now appear bold.

13. Finally, spend a few moments experimenting with the **Tell Me** box (for example, try using it to activate the **Italic** and **Underline** commands).

Driving Lesson 8 - Preferences

▣ Park and Read

Basic preferences control how *Excel* works. They can easily be changed and customised on the **Excel Options** dialog box.

↱ Manoeuvres

1. Click the **File** tab, **File** , and then select **Options** on the left. The **Excel Options** dialog box appears that can be used to set and control user preferences.

2. Display each option in turn on the left to view available options on the right. Do <u>not</u> make any changes.

3. Select **General** on the left.

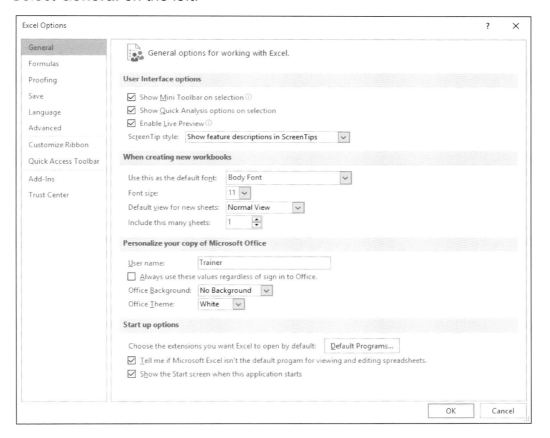

ℹ️ *Your **User name** appears in the file information for every spreadsheet you create. It also appears when you share and work on a spreadsheet with another person.*

4. To change your user details, enter your own name in **User name** (if it is not already).

Driving Lesson 8 - Continued

User name:	John Olivier

i   *Notice that there are also options available here to change the **Office Background** picture and **Office Theme** (colours).*

5.   Next, select **Save** on the left.

6.   Note that the **Default local file location** is the **Documents** folder. This is the default location that will appear when you try to open or save a new spreadsheet.

> ☑ Save to Computer by default
>
> Default local file location: C:\Users\Trainer\Documents
>
> Default personal templates location:

i   *The file path that appears will be different on your computer.*

i   *Notice the **Save to Computer by default** option. If this is <u>not</u> selected, the default open and save location will be your **OneDrive** folder online.*

7.   Leave the **Default local file location** as it is for now.

8.   Click **Customize Ribbon** on the left. The options that appear allow you to add or remove tabs, buttons and groups on the **Ribbon**. Do not do this now.

9.   Click **Quick Access Toolbar** on the left. The options that appear allow you to add or remove buttons on the **Quick Access Toolbar**. Again, do not do this now.

10.   Click **OK** to save changes and close the **Excel Options** dialog box.

Driving Lesson 9 - Closing Excel

P Park and Read

If any unsaved workbooks are still open when *Excel* is closed, a warning will be displayed with an option to save changes. The two main ways to close *Excel* are:

a) Use the **Close** button, ✕, in the top right corner of the screen
b) Use the key press <**Alt F4**>

Manoeuvres

1. A blank worksheet is still displayed on-screen. Click the **Close** button, ✕, in the top right corner of the screen.

2. As you have not saved the current workbook yet, you may be prompted to do so.

3. If the above message appears, select **Don't Save**. The workbook is closed <u>without</u> saving and *Excel* is closed.

4. Start *Excel* again and create a new **Blank workbook**.

5. Close *Excel* with the key press <**Alt F4**>. The current workbook is closed and *Excel* closes.

ℹ️ *A prompt to save changes only appears if you have changed an open worksheet or adjusted any formatting options.*

Driving Lesson 10 - Revision

▣ Park and Read

At the end of every section you get the chance to complete one or more revision exercises to develop your skills and prepare you for your ECDL certification test. You should aim to complete the following steps without referring back to the previous lessons.

↱ Manoeuvres

1. Start *Excel* and create a new **Blank workbook**.

2. How is the **Active Cell** displayed?

3. How many worksheets are there in a new workbook by default?

4. Use the mouse pointer to find **ToolTips** for the following buttons, located on the **Home** tab:

   a)

   b)

   c)

   d)

5. How many groups are displayed on the **Data** tab on the **Ribbon**?

6. The **Formulas** tab has the following groups: **Function Library**, **Defined Names**, **Formula Auditing** and which other?

7. Close *Excel*. What is the button called that actually closes the application down?

ℹ *Sample answers can be found at the back of the guide.*

Driving Lesson 11 - Revision

☞ Manoeuvres

1. Start *Excel*.

2. What function does the key combination <**Alt F4**> perform?

3. How many buttons are on the **Quick Access Toolbar**, by default, and what are they called?

4. With a key press move to the last column on the worksheet, **XFD**. What did you press?

5. Move down to the last row on the worksheet. What is the row number?

6. Return to cell **A1** with a key press. What did you press?

7. Use the **Tell Me** box to search for **shortcuts**. Find a help topic on keyboard shortcuts in *Excel* and read it.

8. Close the help window.

9. Use the **Tell Me** box to find a command to **Align Right** text in the selected cell. Select this to apply the formatting.

10. Close *Excel* without saving changes to any worksheet.

ⓘ *Sample answers can be found at the back of the guide.*

ⓘ *Now complete the **Record of Achievement Matrix** at the back of the guide. You should only move on when confident with the topics and features described in this section.*

Section 2
Open and Close
Workbooks

By the end of this section you should be able to:

Open a Workbook

Open Multiple Workbooks

Use Scroll Bars

Close a Workbook

Work through the **Driving Lessons** in this section to gain an understanding of the above features.

For each **Driving Lesson**, read all of the **Park and Read** instructions and then perform the numbered steps of the **Manoeuvres**. Complete the **Revision** exercise(s) at the end of the section to test your knowledge.

Driving Lesson 12 - Opening a Workbook

🅿 Park and Read

Saved workbooks can easily be opened to use again.

⤵ Manoeuvres

1. Start *Excel* and the welcome screen appears. A list of recently used spreadsheets, if available, appear on the left.

2. For now, click **Open Other Workbooks** to display the **Open** screen.

3. Click **This PC** and then click **Browse**. The **Open** dialog box appears. Navigate to the location where the data files for this guide are stored.

ℹ️ *This guide assumes that the folder being used for the storage of files is* **Documents \ DATA FILES \ ECDL \ Spreadsheet Software**. *If this is not the case, simply select the appropriate folder.*

4. The location for the save is shown at the top of the dialog box. Double click on **DATA FILES** to open the folder.

5. Then double click **ECDL**.

6. Finally, double click **Spreadsheet Software** to display the data files used with this guide.

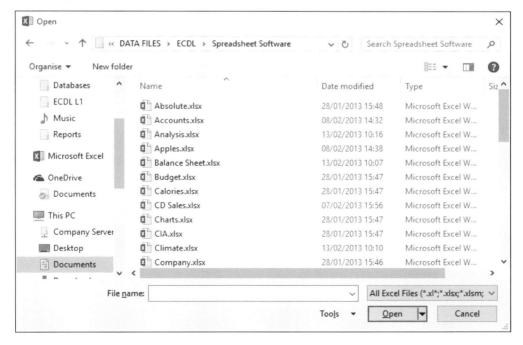

7. If your files do not appear as above, change the view to **Details** using the **Views** drop-down button, ⬚ , on the toolbar.

Driving Lesson 12 - Continued

8.   In the list of files, click once on **Hotel** – the workbook to be opened.

*Excel can find files by starting to type their name in the **File name** box. Select from the list that appears and then click **Open**. This action saves time when faced with a folder with a large number of files.*

9.   Click the **Open** button. The **Hotel** workbook is opened.

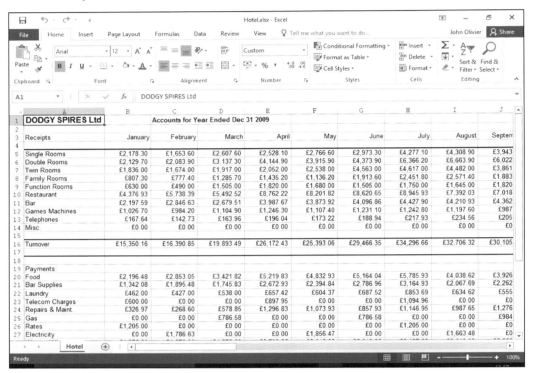

*Files can also be opened by double clicking them in the **Open** dialog box or from Windows **File Explorer**.*

10.   Leave the **Hotel** workbook open for the next lesson.

Driving Lesson 13 - Closing a Workbook

▣ Park and Read

If a workbook is to no longer to be used at this time, it needs to be closed.

⤷ Manoeuvres

1. The workbook **Hotel** should still be on the screen from the previous lesson. If not, open it.

2. Click the **File** tab and then **Close** to close the workbook. The following dialog box may be displayed to prevent the accidental loss of the changes.

3. If the above message does appear, click **Don't Save** which will close the file <u>without</u> saving.

*ℹ️ The key press <**Ctrl W**> can also be used to close the active window.*

4. There should be no **Workbooks** open. The centre part of the screen is blank and most of the buttons are ghosted.

*ℹ️ If a blank workbook is still displayed, close it by clicking the **File** tab and selecting **Close**.*

Driving Lesson 14 - Using Scroll Bars

▣ Park and Read

Small movements between adjacent cells are usually achieved using the cursor keys. However, when moving to a different area of the worksheet, the mouse and **Scroll Bars** are used.

⮕ Manoeuvres

1. Click the **File** tab and select **Open** (or use the key press <**Ctrl O**>). The **Open** screen is displayed again.

2. Click **This PC** and then **Browse**. In the data files folder for this guide, open the workbook **Oscars**.

3. Click on cell **C3** to make it the **Active Cell**.

4. The screen has a horizontal and vertical scroll bar that can be used to scroll the worksheet.

5. Click the down arrow of the vertical scroll bar to view more of the worksheet by one row. Continue to do this until row **6** is at the top of the screen. If you go too far this can be reversed by clicking on the up arrow.

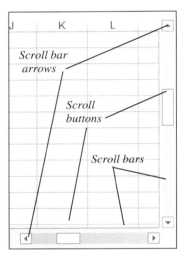

6. Click the right arrow of the horizontal scroll bar to view one more column of the worksheet. Continue to do this until column **D** is at the left of the screen.

7. Notice that the **Active Cell Reference** field still reads **C3**. Even though it is not currently on the screen, **C3** is still the **Active Cell**.

8. To move a whole screen view down, click once on the vertical scroll bar between the scroll button and the bottom arrow. To move a whole screen view to the right, click once on the horizontal scroll bar between the scroll button and the right arrow.

9. Now click the vertical scroll button and drag it up slowly a small amount. The work area scrolls continuously up until the mouse button is released.

10. Drag the horizontal scroll button to the left. The work area scrolls horizontally. Use the scroll buttons to view cell **A1**, then click on cell **B3** to make it the active cell.

11. Use the scroll buttons to scroll to the right and down as far as possible. Press <**Enter**>, this moves the active cell down to **B4**. The worksheet view will reset so that the new active cell, **B4** is displayed.

12. Close the workbook <u>without</u> saving.

Driving Lesson 15 - Opening Multiple Workbooks

Park and Read

More than one workbook can be open at the same time.

Manoeuvres

1. Open the workbook **Spires**.

2. Without closing the **Spires** workbook, use the **File** tab to open the workbook **Grades**.

3. Two workbooks are now open. Click on the **Excel** button on the **Taskbar**. Previews of each open workbook are listed above the button.

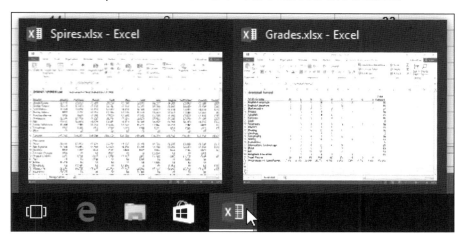

4. Notice how the preview for the workbook **Grades** is highlighted slightly, showing that it is the currently active workbook.

5. Click the **Spires** preview to view that workbook. This workbook is now active.

6. Use the **File** tab to open the workbook **Budget**. The **Excel** button now, when clicked, shows three workbooks in the list.

7. Which workbook, after clicking the **Excel** button on the **Taskbar**, is highlighted?

ℹ️ *The key press <**Alt Tab**> can be used to switch from window to window.*

8. Display **Spires**.

9. Close all the open workbooks <u>without</u> saving.

ℹ️ *Answers are shown in the **Answers** section at the end of this guide.*

Driving Lesson 16 - Revision

▣ Park and Read

At the end of every section you get the chance to complete one or more revision exercises to develop your skills and prepare you for your ECDL certification test. You should aim to complete the following steps without referring back to the previous lessons.

⌐ Manoeuvres

1. Open the workbook **Hotel**.

2. Use the scroll bars to view all of the spreadsheet.

3. Make **A1** the active cell in the **Hotel** workbook.

4. Scroll down with the scroll button to display **Row 15** as the first row on the screen.

5. Leave the **Hotel** workbook open and open the workbook **Grades**.

6. Make **Hotel** the active workbook.

7. Close the workbook **Hotel** <u>without</u> saving.

8. Close the workbook **Grades** <u>without</u> saving.

 *Now complete the **Record of Achievement Matrix** at the back of the guide. You should only move on when confident with the topics and features described in this section.*

Section 3
Creating and Saving
Workbooks

By the end of this section you should be able to:

Start a New Workbook

Enter Text and Numbers

Save a New and Named Workbook

Save Workbooks in Different Formats

Save a Workbook as a Template

Work through the **Driving Lessons** in this section to gain an understanding of the above features.

For each **Driving Lesson**, read all of the **Park and Read** instructions and then perform the numbered steps of the **Manoeuvres**. Complete the **Revision** exercise(s) at the end of the section to test your knowledge.

Driving Lesson 17 - Starting a New Workbook

▣ Park and Read

A workbook based on the default **Blank workbook** template must be started to begin creating a new spreadsheet.

↱ Manoeuvres

1.   Start a new workbook by clicking the **File** tab and selecting **New**.

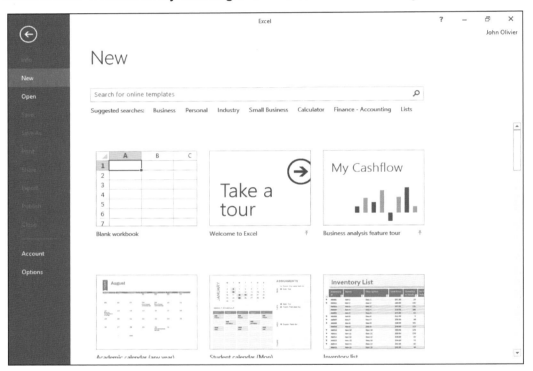

2.   A **Blank workbook** is the first template type. This is the template you should always use to start a new, empty workbook.

i *A template is a ready-made workbook that has been created for a specific purpose (e.g. a budget calculator, expenses calculator, address list, inventory list, shopping list). All you need to do is enter your own data – all formatting and cell formulas will have been set-up for you.*

3.   Following this are templates for a variety of other uses. Scroll down the window to see what is available.

i *At the top of the window is a **Search for online templates** box that can be used to find more templates online.*

4.   For now, simply click **Blank workbook** to start a new workbook and leave it open for the next lesson.

Driving Lesson 18 - Entering Labels

Park and Read

Labels describe the contents of a worksheet and are often used as column or row titles. When entering information into a cell, notice that the text appears in the **Formula Bar** as well as in the cell. A cell should really only ever contain one data item, e.g. a first name in one cell and a surname in an adjacent cell. This makes the data much easier to manipulate and sort. It is also good practice when creating a list of data to make sure it is easy to read. You can use a variety of layouts to do this: leave cells surrounding a list blank, leave a blank row before a row showing totals, and so on. Make sure you don't leave blank rows or columns in the list of data itself though.

Manoeuvres

1. With a blank workbook on screen, click on cell **A3** to select it.

2. Type the label **Fruit**. Notice **ENTER** appears on the **Status Bar**, and that the **Enter** button appears in the **Formula Bar**. Press the <**Enter**> key to place the label into cell **A3**.

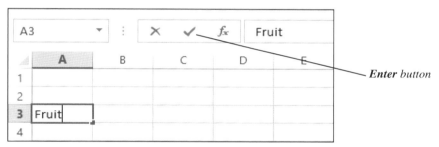

*The entry can also be completed by clicking on the **Enter** button.*

3. Move to cell **B3** and type **Apples**. Place **Apples** in **B3** by pressing the right cursor key →. This automatically enters the data into **B3** and moves the active cell to the right, ready for the next entry.

4. Pressing <**Enter**> moves the selection down, by default. Click the **File** tab and then click **Options**. Display the **Advanced** options and check that the **Direction** is **Down** under **After pressing Enter, move selection**. Click **OK**.

	A	B	C	D	E
1					
2					
3	Fruit	Apples	Pears	Oranges	Total
4	Jan				
5	Feb				
6	Mar				
7	Total				
8					

    Complete the entries into the cells as opposite. If any mistakes are made, leave the errors.

5. Leave the workbook open for the next lesson.

Driving Lesson 19 - Entering Numbers

▣ Park and Read

Numbers must begin with one of the following characters: **0 1 2 3 4 5 6 7 8 9 . + -** or a currency symbol.

↱ Manoeuvres

1. Use the workbook from the previous lesson.

2. Click on cell **B4** and type **36**, followed by **<Enter>**. The active cell is placed in cell **B5** ready for the next entry.

3. Enter the rest of the information into the correct cells, using the cursor movement keys to complete each entry.

	A	B	C	D	E	F
1						
2						
3	Fruit	Apples	Pears	Oranges	Total	
4	Jan	36	38	26		
5	Feb	40	26	37		
6	Mar	53	20	41		
7	Total					
8						

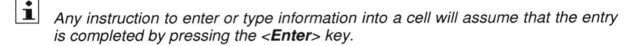 *Any instruction to enter or type information into a cell will assume that the entry is completed by pressing the <**Enter**> key.*

4. Do **NOT** close the workbook as it is saved in a later lesson.

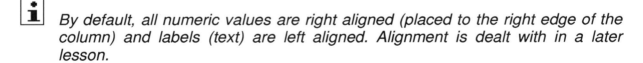 *By default, all numeric values are right aligned (placed to the right edge of the column) and labels (text) are left aligned. Alignment is dealt with in a later lesson.*

Driving Lesson 20 - Saving a New Workbook

▣ Park and Read

After creating a worksheet, it needs to be saved as a workbook so it can be used again. The **Save** process includes selecting the location to save to, giving the workbook a name and selecting the type of format to save it in.

↱ Manoeuvres

1. With the worksheet open from the last lesson, click the **Save** button, 🖫, on the **Quick Access Toolbar**.

ℹ️ *Or click the **File** tab and select **Save As**; or use the key press <**Ctrl S**>.*

2. The **Save As** screen appears. Click **This PC** then **Browse**. Navigate to the data files folder for this guide.

3. Click once in the **File name** box and type **Fruit** to change the default workbook name.

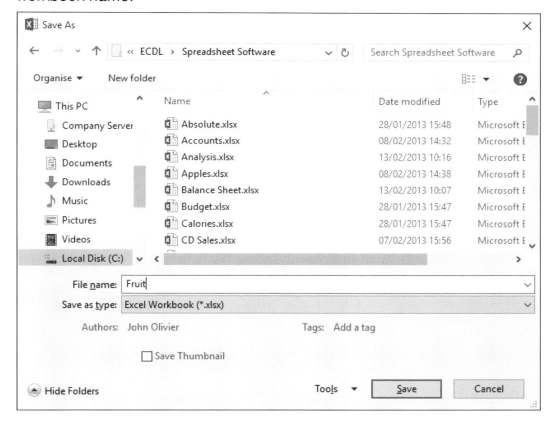

4. Click the **Save** button to save the file, then check the **Title Bar** for the file name.

5. Leave the workbook **Fruit** open.

Driving Lesson 21 - Saving a Named Workbook

▣ Park and Read

There are two commands used when saving a workbook.

Save   saves the file under the same name as previously used and overwrites the earlier version.

Save As   saves the workbook as a different file, creating a different version than the original. This option can be used to create a backup of a file to another location, e.g. a memory stick.

⟳ Manoeuvres

1. The workbook **Fruit** should still be on-screen from the last lesson. Select cell **A1**, type your name, then press <**Enter**> to complete the entry.

2. This workbook will now be saved as **Fruit2**. Click the **File** tab and select **Save As** on the left.

3. With **This PC** selected, notice the **Current Folder** list on the right. Does it contain a link to the **Spreadsheet Software** folder?

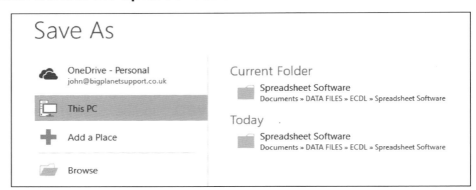

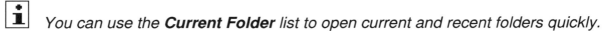
*You can use the **Current Folder** list to open current and recent folders quickly.*

4. Use either the **Current Folder** list or the **Browse** button to view the **Save As** dialog box. Make sure the data files folder for this guide is selected.

5. Change the **File name** to **Fruit2** to save the file with the new name. Click **Save**.

6. The file is now saved with a new name. Close the workbook **Fruit2**.

7. Display the **File** tab and then, with **Open** selected on the left, open the file **Fruit** again. The workbook appears as saved earlier (without your name).

*You can use the "recently used" list on the right of the **Save As** screen to open past workbooks quickly.*

8. Close the workbook **Fruit**.

Driving Lesson 22 - Saving in Different Formats

▣ Park and Read

Workbooks can be saved in a variety of formats including plain text, workbook template, or older versions of *Excel*.

↰ Manoeuvres

1. Open the workbook **Grades**. This workbook cannot be opened in older versions of *Excel* or other programs without being saved in the correct format. To save the workbook in a different format, click the **File** tab, select **Save As**, then open the **Spreadsheet Software** folder.

2. On the **Save As** dialog box, enter **Test Format** in the **File Name** box and click the **Save as type** box.

3. Scan the list to see all the available formats that *Excel* can use. Choose the **Excel 97-2003 Workbook**, a set of previous *Excel* versions. Click **Save**. The workbook is saved as **Test Format.xls**.

Excel Workbook (*.xlsx)
Excel Macro-Enabled Workbook (*.xlsm)
Excel Binary Workbook (*.xlsb)
Excel 97-2003 Workbook (*.xls)
XML Data (*.xml)
Single File Web Page (*.mht;*.mhtml)
Web Page (*.htm;*.html)
Excel Template (*.xltx)
Excel Macro-Enabled Template (*.xltm)
Excel 97-2003 Template (*.xlt)
Text (Tab delimited) (*.txt)
Unicode Text (*.txt)
XML Spreadsheet 2003 (*.xml)
Microsoft Excel 5.0/95 Workbook (*.xls)
CSV (Comma delimited) (*.csv)
Formatted Text (Space delimited) (*.prn)
Text (Macintosh) (*.txt)
Text (MS-DOS) (*.txt)
CSV (Macintosh) (*.csv)
CSV (MS-DOS) (*.csv)
DIF (Data Interchange Format) (*.dif)
SYLK (Symbolic Link) (*.slk)
Excel Add-In (*.xlam)
Excel 97-2003 Add-In (*.xla)
PDF (*.pdf)
XPS Document (*.xps)
OpenDocument Spreadsheet (*.ods)

4. To save the file in a format that can be opened in other applications, display the **Save As** dialog box again and, from the **Save as type**, select **CSV (Comma delimited)**. Click **Save**.

5. If a workbook contains features that are not supported in the chosen format, a message is displayed about losing formatting. Click **Yes**. The workbook is saved as **Test Format.csv**.

6. To save the workbook in *OpenDocument* format (another spreadsheet application), display the **Save As** dialog box and, from **Save as type**, select **OpenDocument Spreadsheet**. Click **Save** and select **Yes** at the prompt. The workbook is saved as **Test Format.ods**. This file can be opened in other applications that support it, e.g. *OpenOffice*.

7. To save the workbook as a simple text file, display the **Save As** dialog box and, from **Save as type**, select **Text (Tab delimited)**. Click **Save** and select **Yes** at the prompt. The workbook is saved as **Test Format.txt**. This text file can be opened in *Notepad*, *WordPad* or *Word*.

8. Close the workbook (click **Don't Save** if prompted).

Driving Lesson 23 - Saving as a Template

🄿 Park and Read

An *Excel* workbook can be saved as a **Template** so that it can be used as a starting point for future workbooks.

↱ Manoeuvres

1. Open the workbook **Scores**. To save this as a template, click the **File** tab, select **Save As** and then select the **Spreadsheet Software** folder.

2. In the **Save As** dialog box, select **Excel Template** from **Save as type**.

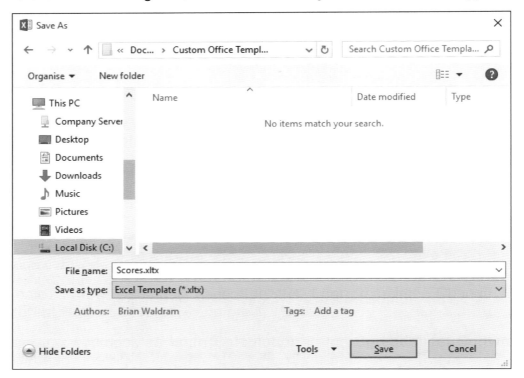

ℹ️ *A **Template** is a base workbook that is stored with other templates. They have an .xltx extension and are shown with a* 🗟 *, icon. They are stored in a* **Custom Office Templates** *folder within* **Documents**.

3. Click **Save** and then close the workbook.

4. To create a workbook based on your new template, display the **File** tab, select **New**, and click **PERSONAL**. Available templates will be displayed.

5. Click your new template, **Scores**. A new workbook based on the template appears. You could do this as many times as you like, using the same **Scores** template as a starting point for new workbooks. Try it!

6. When you are finished, close all open workbooks (without saving).

Driving Lesson 24 - Revision

▣ Park and Read

At the end of every section you get the chance to complete one or more revision exercises to develop your skills and prepare you for your ECDL certification test. You should aim to complete the following steps without referring back to the previous lessons.

↱ Manoeuvres

1. Start with a new, blank workbook.

2. Create the following worksheet in the columns and rows indicated.

	A	B	C	D	E	F
1	Fred Bloggs					
2						
3	Number	Add	Subtract	Multiply	Divide	
4	First	6	7	5	12	
5	Second	3	4	3	4	
6	Result					
7						

3. Save the workbook as **Maths** to the **Spreadsheet Software** folder and close it.

4. Start a new workbook and create the following worksheet:

	A	B	C	D
1	Formatting Section			
2				
3	Exercise	Title		
4	39	General Formatting		
5	40	Format Cells		
6	41	Format Number		
7	42	Date and Time		
8	43	Alignment		
9	44	Wrap Text		
10	45	Merge Cells		
11	46	Text Orientation		
12	47	Borders		
13	48	Revision		
14				

5. Save the workbook as **Formatting Section** and close it.

Driving Lesson 25 - Revision

Manoeuvres

1. Start with a new, blank workbook.

2. Create the following worksheet in the columns and rows indicated.

	A	B	C	D	E	F	G	H	I
1	Satellite Sales Figures								
2									
3		Mon	Tue	Wed	Thu	Fri	Sat	Sun	Total
4	Zara	0	3	5	3	2	4	5	
5	George	4	5	3	0	7	6	2	
6	Ishmael	3	2	0	6	4	5	3	
7	Liz	3	6	2	4	5	10	0	
8	Total								
9									

3. Save the workbook as **Satellite**.

4. Save the workbook as **Satellite2003** in a worksheet format that can be opened in **Excel 2003**.

5. Close the workbook **Satellite2003**.

6. Open the workbook **Quickloan**.

7. Save the worksheet as an **Excel Template** with the name **Loan**.

8. Close the workbook.

9. Create a new workbook based on the **Loan** template. Change the **Interest Rate** in **C3** to **10%** and press <**Enter**>.

10. Save the workbook as **Loan Calculation** in the **Spreadsheet Software** folder and close it.

11. Create another new workbook based on the **Loan** template. Notice that none of the changes made in step 10 have affected the template.

12. Close the workbook without saving and open the workbook **Calories**.

13. Enter your name in **A3** and test the calories counter using your own details.

14. Save the workbook as **Calorie Intake**.

15. Close the workbook.

*Now complete the **Record of Achievement Matrix** at the back of the guide. You should only move on when confident with the topics and features described in this section.*

Section 4
Formulas

By the end of this section you should be able to:

Enter Basic Formulas

Use AutoSum

Check Formulas

Check Spelling

Work through the **Driving Lessons** in this section to gain an understanding of the above features.

For each **Driving Lesson**, read all of the **Park and Read** instructions and then perform the numbered steps of the **Manoeuvres**. Complete the **Revision** exercise(s) at the end of the section to test your knowledge.

Driving Lesson 26 - Formulas

⊞ Park and Read

A calculation in *Excel* is called a **Formula**.

All formulas begin with an equals = sign, followed by the calculation. The calculation consists of cell references or numbers separated by a mathematical symbol (+ add, - subtract, * multiply, / divide), e.g. **=A1+A2**.

Formulas are used to calculate answers from numbers that are entered onto a sheet. To create formulas properly you should enter the cell references of those cells used in the calculation rather than just typing in the numbers. This means that if the numbers in these cells are changed later, the formulas will be recalculated and will still be correct.

⌒ Manoeuvres

1. Start a new workbook, select cell **B2** and type in **66**. Move to cell **B3** and type **34**.

2. Move to cell **B4** and enter a formula to add the contents of cells **B2** and **B3** by typing **=b2+b3**. Press <**Enter**>. Click in cell **B4** and note the cell display of **100** and the formula in the **Formula Bar** converts to uppercase.

3. In **B6** enter the formula which divides B2 by B3: **=b2/b3**. Press <**Enter**> to confirm the entry and the answer is shown as **1.941176**.

4. Move to cell **A8** and enter the following numbers (use the right directional arrow to complete each entry) into these cells: A8 **35,** B8 **23,** C8 **56,** D8 **99,** E8 **55**.

5. Move to cell **F8** and type in this formula **=a8+b8+c8+d8+e8** and press <**Enter**>. The answer should be **268**.

6. Move back to cell **F8** and enter an = sign to begin the formula. Select cell **A8** and it appears in the **Formula Bar**. Type in the **+** symbol, then select cell **B8**. Continue entering the **+** symbol and selecting the other cells until the formula **=A8+B8+C8+D8+E8** is complete again. Note the different coloured cell borders that match the cell references. Press <**Enter**>.

7. Move to cell **B8** and change the value to **43** by over-typing the original value. Press <**Enter**> and the formula in cell **F8** is instantly recalculated. A spreadsheet containing formulas is never out of date.

8. Leave the workbook open for the next lesson.

Driving Lesson 27 - Brackets

Park and Read

When more than one symbol is used in a formula, then the order becomes important, e.g. **A1+A2/A3**. *Excel* performs calculations in this order: **B**rackets over **D**ivision, **M**ultiplication, **A**ddition and finally **S**ubtraction (the **BODMAS** theory).

Manoeuvres

1. Click the **New Sheet** button, ⊕, to the right of **Sheet1** (there can be more than one worksheet in each workbook, clicking on a **Sheet** tab displays that sheet).

2. Create the following small worksheet.

3. To calculate the profit, click on cell **B5** and type the formula **=b2-b3*b4** and press <**Enter**> to complete the formula.

4. The answer is given as **-14** because multiplication is carried out before the subtraction (according to the **BODMAS** theory).

5. Click on cell **B5** to re-enter the formula, but this time add brackets around the subtraction part of the formula **=(b2-b3)*b4**. The old formula is replaced by the new.

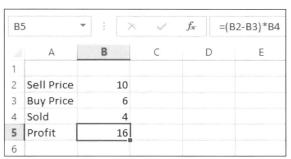

6. Check the answer displayed. Profit per item **10-6**, which is **4**, multiplied by the number sold, **4**, giving **16**.

7. Close the workbook <u>without</u> saving the changes.

ℹ️ *Brackets are added to force* **Excel** *to perform calculations in a different order. The calculation in the brackets will be performed first no matter what mathematical operation is used.*

Driving Lesson 28 - AutoSum

▣ Park and Read

The most common mathematical operation is addition. This calculation can been simplified by the use of a **Function** called **AutoSum**. **AutoSum** adds the contents of cells automatically.

AutoSum, $\boxed{\Sigma \cdot}$, can be found on two **Ribbon** tabs: **Home** and **Formulas**. The **Home** tab has a button in the **Editing** group and on the **Formulas** tab there is an **AutoSum** button in the **Function Library** group.

⤵ Manoeuvres

1. Start a new workbook and enter the following numbers into the cells shown:

	A	B	C	D	E
1					
2		2	1	3	
3		3	5	2	
4		4	2	1	
5					

2. Select cell **B5** and click the **AutoSum** button, $\boxed{\Sigma \text{ AutoSum } \cdot}$, on the **Formulas** tab (within the **Function Library** group). The **AutoSum** feature automatically finds numbers to add.

	A	B	C	D	E
1					
2		2	1	3	
3		3	5	2	
4		4	2	1	
5		=SUM(B2:B4)			
6		SUM(**number1**, [number2], ...)			
7					

3. Press <**Enter**> to complete the entry. The answer should be **9**. Repeat this in cells **C5** and **D5**.

4. **AutoSum** also adds cells across. Select cell **E2** and click the **AutoSum** button. Press <**Enter**> to complete the entry. Repeat this in **E3** and **E4**.

5. Close the workbook without saving.

6. Open the workbook **Sum**.

7. Select cell **B7**. The three numbers above need to be added together to find the total number of apples sold in the three month period.

Driving Lesson 28 - Continued

8.   Click the **AutoSum** button, [∑ AutoSum ▾]

9.   Finish the formula by pressing <**Enter**> to sum the numbers above. The answer should be **129**.

10. Move to cell **E4** and click the **AutoSum** button, [∑ AutoSum ▾]. The January figures are selected, so press <**Enter**> to complete the formula. The answer should be **100**.

11. Use **AutoSum** to calculate the totals in cells, **C7**, **D7** and **E5**.

> **i** *AutoSum adds the cells above or left depending on where nearby figures are located. If **AutoSum** has figures in both directions it will sum the cells above by default.*

12. Use **AutoSum** to calculate the total in cell **E6**. After clicking [∑ AutoSum ▾] you will need to click and drag with the mouse from cell **B6** to cell **D6** to select the range **B6:D6**, as the cells above **E6** are selected by default. Complete the formula by pressing <**Enter**>.

13. Calculate the grand total in cell **E7** (adding cells to the left or above displays the same result, so the default range will be correct).

14. The answer **317** appears.

15. Save the workbook as **Sum Complete** and close it.

Driving Lesson 29 - Checking for Errors

▣ Park and Read

A worksheet is of little use if one formula within it is incorrect. Correct spelling is also important. It is vital that workbooks that are to be distributed are checked so that the worksheets contain no text or formula errors.

Formulas must be checked to see that they refer to the correct cells. Some formulas produce **#MESSAGE** denoting an error. Types of errors you need to recognise are:

#DIV/0!	Division by zero
#REF!	Cell reference is not valid
#NAME?	Does not recognise text in a formula

You may also come across the following errors:

#NULL!	The two areas specified do not intersect
#VALUE!	The wrong argument used
#NUM!	Error with number in formula
#N/A	The value used in the formula is not available
######	The result is too long to fit into the cell

Mistakes can be checked either visually or, better still, using *Excel's* spell checking facility.

⌒ Manoeuvres

1. Start a new workbook.

2. In cell **B3** type **6**, in cell **D3** type **8**, in cell **B5** type **10** and in cell **D5** enter the formula **=b3+b5-d3**. Press <**Enter**>.

3. Double click on cell **D5** to check the formula.

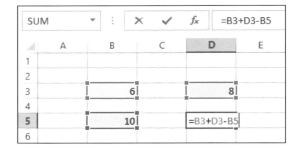

 Excel uses a different colour for each part of the formula.

4. If your screen matches the above diagram then it is correct. Press <**Enter**>.

5. Close the workbook <u>without</u> saving.

Driving Lesson 29 - Continued

6.   Open the workbook **Formulas**. Check the formulas on row **6** and cell **B12** for errors by double clicking on each cell. Remember to press <**Esc**> to cancel after checking.

7.   There is an error in cell **D6** – it contains a value, not a formula. Enter a formula in cell **D6** to multiply the two numbers above, **=d4*d5**.

8.   Click on cell **E5** and enter **0**. The cell **E6** displays the **#DIV/0!** error message, division by zero. Click on cell **E6** and display the **Formulas** tab.

9.   Click the **Error Checking** button, in the **Formula Auditing** group. The error is described in the **Error Checking** dialog box. Read the information. Experiment with the options and then close It.

10.   Close the workbook <u>without</u> saving.

11.   Open the workbook **Spell**. With **A1** the active cell, click the **Review** tab and click the **Spelling** button, in the **Proofing** group.

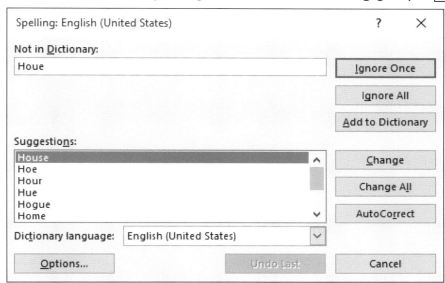

12.   The **Spelling** dialog box will show the first mistake. **A1** is highlighted. The cell should read **House**. The **Suggestions** box displays **House**, so click the **Change** button to correct the error.

13.   The **Spelling** dialog box finds the next mistake in cell **A4**. The cell should read **Other**, the **h** has been missed out. Click on **Other** in the **Suggestions** list and then click the **Change** button. Correct the other mistakes on the worksheet.

> *Text can be entered directly into the **Not in Dictionary** box, if the required word is not in the **Suggestions** list, or, the error can be ignored.*

14.   When finished spell checking, click **OK**.

15.   Close the workbook <u>without</u> saving.

Driving Lesson 30 - Revision

▣ Park and Read

At the end of every section you get the chance to complete one or more revision exercises to develop your skills and prepare you for your ECDL certification test. You should aim to complete the following steps without referring back to the previous lessons.

↱ Manoeuvres

1. On a blank worksheet enter the numbers in the cells to match below.

◢	A	B	C	D	E	F
1					4	
2					7	
3					5	
4					2	
5					4	
6					3	
7					8	
8					9	
9	8	2	4	7		
10						

2. Click in cell **E9**. **AutoSum** is to be used. Will it sum the column or the row?

3. Click the **AutoSum** button on the **Home** tab. Press <**Enter**>. What is the answer?

4. Delete the answer in cell **E9** by clicking in cell **E9** and pressing the <**Delete**> key. You now need to sum the row of numbers. Click the **AutoSum** button, then click and drag from **A9** to **D9** or **D9** to **A9**. Press <**Enter**> to complete the formula. What is the answer?

5. Click on cell **E3** and delete the contents.

6. Delete the answer in **E9**.

7. With cell **E9** active click the **AutoSum** button. You need to add all the column, click and drag the range **E1:E8**, press <**Enter**>. What is the answer?

8. Close the workbook without saving it.

ℹ️ *Sample answers can be found at the back of the guide.*

Driving Lesson 31 - Revision

⌐ Manoeuvres

1. Start a new workbook. The worksheet below contains data on boxes of fruit. Insert the following information in the cells indicated.

◢	A	B	C	D	E
1					
2					
3	Fruit	Apples	Pears	Oranges	Total
4	Jan	6	8	12	
5	Feb	7	6	10	
6	Mar	11	5	9	
7	Total				
8	Sell Price				
9	Income				
10	Buy Price				
11	Profit				
12					

2. Use **AutoSum** to sum the sales for each fruit (in **Row 7**) and for each month (in **Column E**). Calculate a grand total in cell **E7** (using either the column totals to the left or the row totals above).

3. The **Sell Price** of the three fruits are **9**, **11** and **13** for the apples, pears and oranges respectively. Enter this information.

4. The **Income** row should contain formulas that multiply the **Total** by the **Sell Price**. Complete the three cells.

5. The buying prices of the three fruits are **5**, **6** and **7** for the apples, pears and oranges respectively. Enter this information.

6. The **Profit** is a more complicated formula containing brackets. Work out the profit for one box of fruit using subtraction in brackets and multiply by the total number of boxes sold. The result in cell **B11** should be **96**.

7. Create similar formulas to calculate the profit for the pears and oranges.

8. Use **AutoSum** to calculate the total income in cell **E9** and total profit in cell **E11**. This should be **377**.

9. Check all the formulas by double clicking on each in turn and then save the completed workbook as **Fruit Sales** and close it.

ℹ️ *Now complete the **Record of Achievement Matrix** at the back of the guide. You should only move on when confident with the topics and features described in this section.*

Section 5 Workbooks

By the end of this section you should be able to:

Use Multiple Worksheets and Workbooks

Switch Between Open Workbooks

Rename Worksheets

Copy and Move Worksheets and Workbooks

Insert and Delete Worksheets

Work through the **Driving Lessons** in this section to gain an understanding of the above features.

For each **Driving Lesson**, read all of the **Park and Read** instructions and then perform the numbered steps of the **Manoeuvres**. Complete the **Revision** exercise(s) at the end of the section to test your knowledge.

Driving Lesson 32 - Multiple Worksheets

▣ Park and Read

A workbook can contain an unlimited number of worksheets, limited only by the available memory. Each sheet must have a different name. This allows related information to be kept together in the same workbook and complicated spreadsheet models to be created.

More than one workbook can be open at the same time. This allows data, sheets and other objects to be copied or moved between workbooks.

⤴ Manoeuvres

1. Open the workbook **CIA**. This is a workbook containing **16** worksheets, representing a company with sixteen area divisions around the country.

2. Notice the sheet tabs across the bottom of the screen. Click on tab **Sheet3**. This makes the sheet active. All 16 sheets cannot be displayed because of the lack of space.

3. There are 2 buttons to the left of **Sheet1**, ◄ ▶ that control the sheet tab display, **Left** and **Right**. Use the **Right** and then **Left** buttons to display different sheet tabs.

4. Hover over the **Right** button. There are commands for showing the last sheet, **<Ctrl+Left click>**, and all sheets (**Right click**).

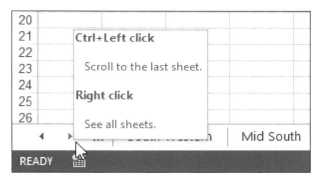

5. Press **<Ctrl+Left click>** to show the tab for **Sheet16**. Click the **Sheet16** tab to make it active, the division name is in cell **B9**.

6. Right click on either the **Left** or **Right** button. All 16 sheets are listed. Select **Sheet5** and click **OK** to activate it.

7. Practise using the sheet display buttons to move around all the sheets.

8. Leave the workbook open for the next lesson.

ℹ️ *To adjust the number of sheets in a default workbook from 1, click the **File** tab, then **Options** and from the **General** options settings, change the value in **Include this many sheets**. Click **OK**.*

Driving Lesson 33 - Switch Between Open Workbooks

▣ Park and Read

More than one workbook can be open at the same time. When a workbook is opened, it is displayed in the active window. Any previously opened workbooks are still open, but are hidden and not active.

↱ Manoeuvres

1. The **CIA** workbook should still be open. If not, open it. Open the workbook **Computer Sales**.

2. By default, each workbook is displayed on the **Taskbar** on the **Excel** button. Hover over the **Excel** button. The active book is highlighted.

3. Slowly move from one workbook to the other. The screen changes to preview the one being pointed at. Move over the **CIA** workbook and click on it to make it active.

ℹ *An alternative method to display a workbook is to click **Switch Windows** on the **View** tab. The open books are shown as a numbered list (the active book has a tick next to it). Selecting a name displays it.*

4. Open the workbook **Climate** and then open **Company**.

5. To display all open workbooks, click **Arrange All** found in the **Window** group on the **View** tab.

6. **Tiled** is the default, so click **OK** to display all open books in a grid pattern.

7. To display a single book, click the **Maximize** button of its window. Click on the **Climate** window and then maximise it.

8. Use **Arrange All** on the **View** tab to display each option in turn: **Horizontal**, **Vertical** and **Cascade**. **Maximise** any window if the **Ribbon** is not displayed.

9. Without saving changes, close **Climate**, then **Company**, then **Computer Sales**. Leave the **CIA** workbook open for the next lesson.

Driving Lesson 34 - Renaming Sheets

▣ Park and Read

The names **Sheet1**, **Sheet2**, etc., are not very helpful for finding information. It makes much more sense to use meaningful names which give a good idea of the content of the worksheet. The sheet tabs can contain up to **31** characters including spaces. Duplicate names are not allowed.

⌒ Manoeuvres

1.   The workbook **CIA** should still be open. **Maximise** the window.

2.   To rename **Sheet1** as **North**, double click the **Sheet1** tab.

3.   Type the new name **North**.

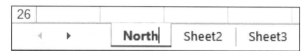

4.   Either press <**Enter**> or click on any cell on the sheet.

  *An alternative method is to use the **Home** tab, **Format** button in the **Cells** group. Select **Rename Sheet**, enter the new name and press <**Enter**>.*

5.   Rename **Sheet2** as **North East**.

6.   Rename all the other sheets with the name of the **Division** in cell **B9**, using any method.

7.   Save the workbook as **Divisions**.

8.   Leave the workbook open for the next lesson.

Driving Lesson 35 - Copying and Moving Sheets

▣ Park and Read

Worksheets can be moved or copied within the same workbook or to a different workbook.

⤷ Manoeuvres

1. The workbook **Divisions** should still be open. If not, open it.

2. Sheets can be moved within the same workbook by dragging the sheet tab with the mouse. Move the **North Midlands** sheet between **South Wales** and **Midlands** by clicking and dragging to the correct position (a black triangle shows where the sheet will be inserted).

3. Move the **North West** sheet between **North** and **North East**.

4. Select the **North** worksheet.

5. An active sheet is copied within the same workbook by holding <**Ctrl**> while dragging its sheet tab. To make a copy of the **North** sheet, hold down <**Ctrl**> then click and drag the **North** sheet tab across to the right, next to **North**. Release the mouse button first before <**Ctrl**>.

ℹ️ *The name of the copied sheet is **North (2)**. Remember duplicate sheet names are not allowed.*

6. If a sheet is to be moved or copied to another workbook a shortcut menu can be used. Right click the **North (2)** sheet tab.

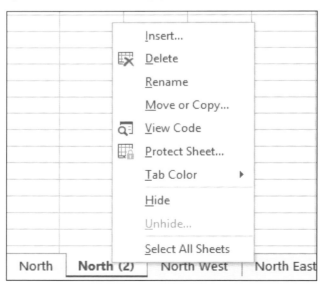

Driving Lesson 35 - Continued

7. This menu controls all the actions relating to sheets. Select **Move or Copy**.

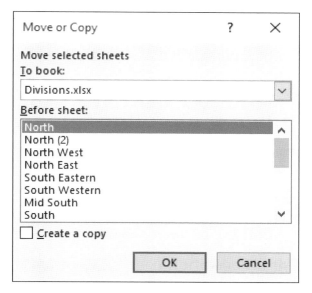

8. To create a copy the **Create a copy** box is checked, otherwise the sheet is moved. Check the **Create a copy** box.

9. To move or copy to a different workbook, a selection is made from the **To book** box. Drop down the list to see the available open workbooks A new workbook is to be created to contain the copied sheet. Select **(new book)**.

*To move or copy to an existing workbook it must be open so it is displayed in the **To book** box.*

10. The **Before sheet** box is empty for a new workbook. An existing one would display all the sheets for a selection to be made on the placement. Click **OK**.

11. A new workbook is created with just the sheet **North (2)** in it. Display the **Divisions** workbook and check that **North (2)** is still in this book and that it was copied.

12. Leave both workbooks open for the next lesson.

Driving Lesson 36 - Inserting and Deleting Sheets

⊞ Park and Read

Once a workbook is open, sheets can be inserted or deleted. The maximum number of sheets in a workbook is limited only by available memory.

⮑ Manoeuvres

1. Two workbooks are open from the previous lesson. The **South** division is to be closed because it is making huge losses. In the **Divisions** workbook, display the **South** sheet tab and then right click on it and select **Delete** from the shortcut menu.

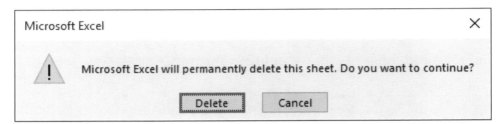

2. Click **Delete** to complete the deletion.

> ℹ️ *An alternative method is to use the **Home** tab, **Delete** drop-down in the **Cells** group. Select **Delete Sheet** and click **Delete**.*

3. The **Midlands** division is also doing poorly. Make **Midlands** active and delete it.

4. Sheets are inserted at the right of the current sheet. A new division called **Western** is to be created and it is to be located before the **Eastern** division. Click the **New Sheet** button, ⊕, located to the right of the sheet tabs. A new sheet is inserted. Move it to be before the **Eastern** sheet.

> ℹ️ *To insert a new worksheet the **Insert** drop-down on the **Home** tab can be used. Select **Insert Sheet**. This command inserts a new worksheet to the left of the active sheet.*

5. Creating a new sheet similar to all the others will take too long. **Delete** the new sheet.

6. Make **Eastern** active and create a copy. The new sheet is named **Eastern (2)**. Rename the sheet and cell **B9** to **Western**.

7. Save the workbook **Divisions** using the same name and then close it.

8. Close the unsaved workbook <u>without</u> saving.

Driving Lesson 37 - Revision

▣ Park and Read

At the end of every section you get the chance to complete one or more revision exercises to develop your skills and prepare you for your ECDL certification test. You should aim to complete the following steps without referring back to the previous lessons.

⬆ Manoeuvres

1.   Open the workbook **Computer Sales**.

2.   Delete the **Sales** sheet.

3.   Copy the **Fruit** sheet to a new workbook.

4.   Save the new workbook as **Copy** and then close it.

5.   Insert a new sheet in **Computer Sales** ready to add more detailed information.

6.   Rename the new sheet **Accounts**.

7.   Display the **Fruit** sheet.

8.   Save the workbook as **Computer Sales2**.

9.   Close the workbook.

 *Now complete the **Record of Achievement Matrix** at the back of the guide. You should only move on when confident with the topics and features described in this section.*

Section 6
Editing

By the end of this section you should be able to:

Edit Data in the Formula Bar and Cells

Delete Cell Contents

Use Undo and Redo

Select Ranges of Data

Use the Fill Handle

Erase and Sort Data

Cut, Copy and Paste

Find and Replace Text

Work through the **Driving Lessons** in this section to gain an understanding of the above features.

For each **Driving Lesson**, read all of the **Park and Read** instructions and then perform the numbered steps of the **Manoeuvres**. Complete the **Revision** exercise(s) at the end of the section to test your knowledge.

Driving Lesson 38 - Editing Cells

🄿 Park and Read

Changes can be made to data in cells in a variety of ways. The easiest way is to overtype one entry with another. When a cell entry is long or complicated small changes are either made in the **Formula Bar** or in the cell itself.

☞ Manoeuvres

1. Open the workbook **CD Sales**.

2. Let's change the text in **B5** (**Quarters**). Click the cell **B5** once.

3. Type the new data label, **Months**, and it replaces **Quarters**.

B5	▾	⋮	✕	✓	*fx*	Months		
⬓ A		B	C	D	E	F	G
1							
2		*CD Sales Ltd.*					
3							
4							
5		Months	First	Second	Third	Fourth	
6		Sales	405	397	376	527	
7		Turnover	£4,050	£3,970	£3,760	£5,270	
8		Profit	£1,012.50	£992.50	£940.00	£1,317.50	
9							

Cancel button (label pointing to the ✕ in the formula bar)

4. Before **<Enter>** is pressed, click the **Cancel** button, ✕ , on the **Formula Bar**. This action cancels the new input, leaving the original data unchanged.

5. Click on cell **C8** and type in **Months**. This time press the **Escape** key, **<Esc>**. This cancels the input and is quicker when typing.

ℹ *These methods to cancel are used when data is accidentally entered into the wrong cell.*

6. Type **Months** into cell **B5** again and press **<Enter>** to complete the entry. The new information replaces the old.

7. Select cell **B7** and notice the cell contents in the **Formula Bar**.

8. Click in the **Formula Bar** and, using the **Backspace** and **Delete** keys to remove the current text, change **Turnover** to **Income**.

Driving Lesson 38 - Continued

9.   Press <**Enter**> to complete the change.

 *When editing cells, the <**Enter**> key must be used to end the process.*

10.   In cell **B8** edit **Profit** to **Gross Profit**.

 The full label cannot be seen. Do not worry about this. Widening columns is covered in a later lesson.

11.   Enter your first name in cell **A1** and complete the entry.

12.   Double click in cell **A1**. A cursor is placed inside the cell to allow editing of the cell contents within the cell. If the cursor is not at the end of your first name, press the <**End**> key. Add a space and then your surname, press <**Enter**> to complete the entry.

13.   Double click in cell **A1** to edit the contents. Click and drag to highlight your first name. Press the <**Delete**> key to remove it. Press <**Enter**> to leave just your surname in the cell.

14.   Close the workbook **CD Sales** <u>without</u> saving.

Driving Lesson 39 - Deleting Cell Contents

▣ Park and Read

Excel allows the user to erase or delete data in many ways. Cell contents are erased using the **Clear Contents** command or by using <**Delete**> on the keyboard.

↰ Manoeuvres

1. On a new, blank worksheet enter the number **1701** into cell **B4** and press <**Enter**>.

2. Select **B4** again.

3. To erase the contents of this cell, click the **Clear** button, , on the **Home** tab, **Editing** group.

4. Select **Clear Contents**.

5. Enter **2000** into cell **B2** and **74656** into **B3**.

6. The **Delete** key can be used to clear contents. Select cell **B2** and then press <**Delete**>. The cell content is now cleared.

7. Clear the contents of cell **B3**.

8. Close the workbook <u>without</u> saving.

Driving Lesson 40 - Using Undo and Redo

▣ Park and Read

As it is so easy to remove the contents of a cell, *Excel* has an **Undo** feature to reverse any mistakes that may have been made. After undoing the action, it can be redone, if necessary, using **Redo**. The **Undo** and **Redo** buttons can be found on the **Quick Access Toolbar**.

Manoeuvres

1. Open the workbook **CD Sales**.

2. Click in cell **E6** and press <**Delete**> to remove the cell contents.

3. Now delete the contents of cell **F6**.

4. Click the **Undo** button, ↰, on the **Quick Access Toolbar**, to reverse the last action, i.e. put the contents back in **F6**.

5. Click the **Undo** button, ↰, again to replace the deletion before last.

6. After undoing an action, it can be *redone* by clicking the **Redo** button. Click the **Redo** button, ↱, to reverse the last action, the **Undo**.

7. Use **Undo** to return the worksheet to its original state.

8. Delete the contents of cells **B5**, **C5**, **D5**, **E5** and **F5** one at a time. All actions that can be undone are stored in the **Undo** history.

9. To use this, click the drop-down arrow on the **Undo** button.

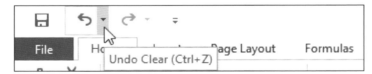

10. Click and drag to **Clear** and **Undo 5 Actions** in one go. The 5 deletions are restored.

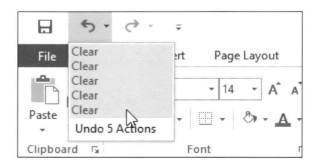

11. Close the workbook **CD Sales** <u>without</u> saving the changes.

Driving Lesson 41 - Ranges

Park and Read

A **range** is a rectangular selection of cells. Just as a single cell is identified by a cell reference, ranges are identified by the cells of their outer limits, e.g. the four cells B2, B3, C2 and C3 is the range **B2:C3**.

Ranges are selected by clicking the mouse button and dragging to highlight multiple cells at the same time (known as **Click and Drag**).

Entire rows, columns, and worksheets can also be selected. Selections are made to allow the highlighted cells to be worked on, i.e. formatted, copied, moved, deleted, etc.

Manoeuvres

1. On a new, blank worksheet click on cell **B2**. Click and drag down and to the right so that a range of six cells is highlighted, as shown below.

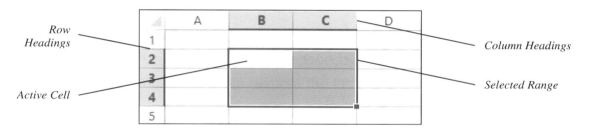

2. Release the mouse button. Notice that the first cell in the range remains white and the other cells are highlighted.

3. Selected ranges can be increased and decreased from the first cell in the range. Hold down the <**Shift**> key and select cell **E7**. The range is increased.

4. Select cell **C2** while holding down <**Shift**> and the range is decreased. Click anywhere on the worksheet to remove the highlighted range.

5. Select the range **B2:C4** again. Press and hold down the <**Ctrl**> key. Click and drag the range **C5:D6**. Release the <**Ctrl**> key.

6. There should now be two separate ranges highlighted. Click anywhere on the sheet to remove the selected ranges.

7. Click the **B** in the **Column Headings**. All cells in column **B** are now highlighted. Click on any cell to remove the selection.

8. Click on **5** in the **Row Headings**. Row **5** is now highlighted. Click on any cell to remove the selection.

9. To select adjacent multiple columns, click in the **Column Headings** and drag to select the required columns. Select columns **C** to **E**.

Driving Lesson 41 - Continued

	A	B	C	D	E	F
1						
2						
3						
4						

10. To select multiple adjacent rows, click and drag in the **Row Headings**. Click and drag from **3** to **5**. Several rows are highlighted.

	A	B	C	D	E
1					
2					
3					
4					
5					
6					

11. Click anywhere to remove the highlighting.

12. Non adjacent rows or columns can be selected using the same technique as for ranges, i.e. hold down the <**Ctrl**> key to select separate parts. Select rows **2** to **5** and **8** to **10**.

	A	B	C	D	E
1					
2					
3					
4					
5					
6					
7					
8					
9					
10					
11					

13. Select columns **B**, **C** and **E**.

14. To select the entire worksheet, click the **Select All** button (to the left of **A** and above **1**).

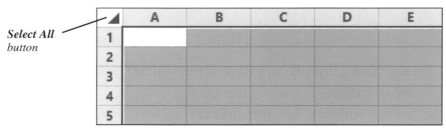

Select All button

15. Click on any cell to remove the highlighting.

Driving Lesson 42 - Using the Fill Handle

Park and Read

The **Fill Handle** quickly copies or increments data to a range of cells. If the data is in the form of days, dates, time, months or text with a number then the **Fill Handle** will increment as it fills, otherwise the data will be copied.

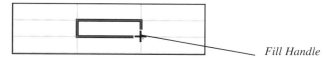

Fill Handle

It is only possible to drag in one direction at one time, i.e. across a row or down a column.

Manoeuvres

1. On the current, blank worksheet, type your first name in cell **B2** and press <**Enter**>.

2. Select **B2** and move the mouse pointer over the fill handle. The cursor changes to a cross-hair, **+**. Click and drag the cell along to **G2**. Your name will be copied into the cells.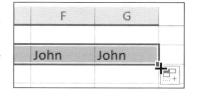

3. Notice that a **Smart Tag** has appeared, ⊞. Click the tag to see what options are available for this operation but do not select any.

4. In **C4** enter **January**. Click and drag the fill handle of **C4** along to **G4**.

5. In **B6** enter today's date in the format **dd/mm/yyyy**.

6. Click and drag the fill handle of **B6** down to **B12**. The default is to increment each date by one day. Click the **Smart Tag** and select the **Fill Years** option. Each date is now incremented by one year.

7. Enter **123** in **D14**. Click and drag the fill handle to **H14**. The entry **123** is repeated.

8. Select **D14** again, hold down the <**Ctrl**> key, and click and drag the fill handle to **H14**. This time the values are incremented.

9. In **J6** enter **10** and in **J7** below enter **15**. Click and drag to highlight the two cells. Use the **Fill Handle** for the selected range to click and drag down to **J12**. The values are incremented by 5 (the difference between the selected numbers in **J6** and **J7**).

10. Experiment using the fill handle with the following examples:

Mon	**9:00 am**	**Order No 999**
1-Jan	**1st Quarter**	**Hello**

11. Close the workbook <u>without</u> saving.

Driving Lesson 43 - Copying Cells

🅿 Park and Read

Rather than repeatedly typing the same data into several cells, the **Copy** command can be used to copy labels, values and formulas. The selected cells are placed in an area of *Windows* called the **Clipboard**, from there they can be **Pasted** to other locations.

↱ Manoeuvres

1. On an new, blank worksheet, click on cell **B3**, type **Hello** then press <**Enter**>.

2. To copy this cell, click on cell **B3** and then click the **Copy** button, 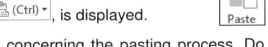.

ℹ *The key press <**Ctrl C**> can be used instead of the **Copy** button.*

ℹ *Excel places a **Marquee** (a moving dashed line) around the selected cell to show which cells are to be copied. Notice that the message **Select destination and press ENTER or choose Paste** is displayed on the **Status Bar**.*

3. Move to cell **B7** and press <**Enter**>. The contents of **B3** will now be pasted into **B7**. The contents of **B3** will remain unchanged. Note that **B3** no longer has a dashed line around it.

4. Enter **65** into **C6** and press <**Enter**>. With **C6** selected, click **Copy**, .

5. Move to **B9** and click the **Paste** button. The value is pasted into the new location and a **Smart Tag**, (Ctrl) ▾, is displayed.

6. Click the tag to see a list of options concerning the pasting process. Do not select any.

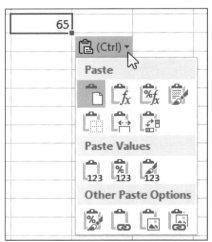

ℹ *The key press <**Ctrl V**> can be used instead of the **Paste** button.*

Driving Lesson 43 - Continued

7. Note that **C6** still has a dashed line, indicating that its contents can be pasted again if required. Move to **B10** and paste again. Press <**Esc**> to end the pasting and remove the dashed line around **C6**.

*The **Paste** command is used for pasting repeatedly, the <**Enter**> key is used to paste a single copy and to end the copy process.*

8. Click the **Clipboard** group launcher on the **Home** tab to display the **Clipboard** task pane.

9. The clipboard is common to all *Office* applications, so it may contain many items already. Click **Clear All** to remove any existing items.

10. To copy a range, highlight the range **B7:B10** and click the **Copy** button. The values will appear in the **Clipboard Task Pane**.

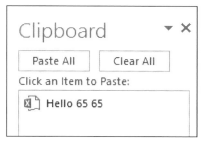

11. As well as using the **Paste** button or the <**Enter**> key, items can be pasted directly from the **Clipboard**. Click the destination cell **H5**, which will become the top left cell of the pasted range, and then click the entry in the **Clipboard**.

*Cells can be copied from sheet to sheet within the same book and can be pasted more than once from the **Clipboard**.*

12. Click the **New Sheet** button, ⊕, to add another worksheet.

13. Click on cell **A2** and then click the entry in the **Clipboard** to paste the range. The four cells from **Sheet1** are copied to **Sheet2**.

14. Click back on **Sheet1** to check that the original range is still present.

15. Close the workbook <u>without</u> saving, but leave the **Clipboard** task pane open.

Driving Lesson 44 - Moving Cells

▣ Park and Read

The **Cut** and **Paste** commands allow the user to <u>move</u> the contents of a cell or a range of cells to other parts of a worksheet, other worksheets or other workbooks.

Care should be taken when moving numbers into cells that are referenced by formulas.

⌐ Manoeuvres

1. Start a new workbook. Note that the **Clipboard** is still displayed.

2. Enter any two numbers in **E5** and **E6**. In **E7** enter a formula to add the two numbers.

3. Select the range **E5:E6**.

4. Click the **Cut** button, ✂, on the **Home** tab to cut the selected cells from the worksheet (they are still there at this point until pasted).

ℹ️ *The key press <**Ctrl X**> can be used instead of the **Cut** button.*

5. Move the pointer to **G7** and click the **Paste** button. The values appear in the new location and disappear from the original cells, i.e. they are moved.

6. Notice that the calculation in **E7** is still correct. Click on cell **E7** to see that the calculation now references the new locations.

ℹ️ *Remember that the key press <**Ctrl V**> can be used instead of the **Paste** button.*

7. In **C8** enter the formula **=c6+c7**. The cell should display zero as the two cells are empty.

8. Select cell **G7** and **G8**, click with the right mouse button and select **Cut** from the shortcut menu.

9. Right click cell **C6** and select **Paste.** The result calculated now shows the **#REF!** error message.

ℹ️ *Take care when pasting into cells that contain data as the original information is overwritten. If cells are referenced by formulas those cells are shown as errors.*

10. Click the **Undo** button to reverse the last paste. Press <**Esc**> to remove the marquee.

Driving Lesson 44 - Continued

11. In cell **G9** use **AutoSum** to add the two numbers (there is an **AutoSum** button, $\boxed{\Sigma \ \cdot}$, in the **Editing** group on the **Home** tab). Press <**Enter**> to confirm the formula and the answer appears.

12. These three cells can be cut or copied and pasted on the same sheet. Highlight the range **G7:G9** and click **Cut**.

13. Click on cell **B3** and use **Paste** to place the three cells. Click on cell **B5** and note the formula references the two cells directly above.

*Cells or ranges that are **Cut** also appear on the **Clipboard** as with the **Copy** function.*

14. As well as moving cells on the same sheet they can also be moved between sheets in the same book. Highlight the range **B3:B5** and click **Cut**.

15. Create a **Sheet2**. Click on cell **H4** and click **Paste**. The cell contents are removed from **Sheet1** and placed on **Sheet2**. Check both **Sheet1** and **Sheet2**.

16. Close the **Clipboard** by clicking the **Close** button.

17. On **Sheet1** delete the cell contents of cell **C8** and **E7**. The sheet should now be blank.

18. Close the open workbook <u>without</u> saving.

Driving Lesson 45 - Copying & Moving between Workbooks

▣ Park and Read

Cell contents can also be copied or moved from workbook to workbook.

↱ Manoeuvres

1. Open the workbooks **League** (world hockey leagues) and **Survey** (an analysis of 220 hockey fans and whether they replied to a survey).

2. A sample of 20 people from the survey has been requested. In the **Survey** workbook, highlight the range **A10:G30** and **Copy** it using any method.

3. Click **Switch Windows** from the **View** tab and click **League** from the drop down list to display the **League** workbook. Alternatively, click the workbook named **League** on the **Taskbar**.

4. Click on the **Sheet2** tab. Click on cell **C5** (the cell to place the copy) and press <**Enter**>. The range is copied from **Survey** to **Sheet2** in the **League** workbook.

ℹ *The data is not fully displayed because the columns are not wide enough. The widening of columns is covered later. Leave it for now.*

5. Make **Survey** the active workbook and close it <u>without</u> saving.

ℹ *Single cells are copied from sheet to sheet and book to book in exactly the same way as a range.*

6. Not only can cells be copied or moved between sheets and open workbooks, they can be moved or copied to a new workbook. Display the workbook **League**, **Sheet1**. Highlight the range **A32:I50** (the last 2 leagues). Select to **Cut**.

7. Start a new workbook and on **Sheet1** make the active cell **A2** and **Paste** the cells. This moves the cells to a different workbook.

8. View the workbook **League** to see the data has been removed from **Sheet1**.

9. Save the new workbook as **Lower Leagues** and close it.

10. Close the workbook **League** <u>without</u> saving.

Driving Lesson 46 - Finding Specific Text

Park and Read

Specific text can be found in formulas, labels, comments, etc. and even replaced if necessary. The search starts at the active cell.

Manoeuvres

1.   Open the workbook **Hotel**.

2.   With **A1** the active cell and the **Home** tab displayed, click the **Find & Select** button in the **Editing** group. Select **Find**.

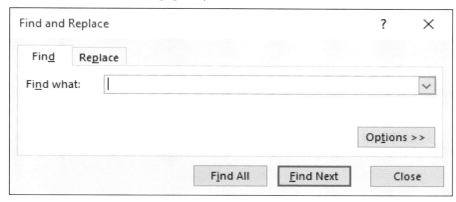

*The **Options** button displays extra options such as whether to search by row or column, whether the text is part or all of the cell content, and whether the text case is important.*

3.   In the **Find what** box, enter **Daily Rate** and click on **Find Next**.

4.   The active cell will now be **R3**, the **Daily Rate**.

*It may be necessary to move the **Find and Replace** dialog box so that the results of the search can be seen.*

5.   Close the **Find and Replace** dialog box and use the key press <**Ctrl Home**> to move back to cell **A1**.

6.   Use the **Find and Replace** dialog box to find the text **Tax**.

7.   The active cell will be **Q22**, the **Tax Rates** label. To find any other occurrences of **Tax**, click on **Find Next**.

8.   The active cell is now **A36**, **Company Tax**. Click **Find Next**. There should be no others. **Close** the dialog box.

9.   Leave the workbook open as it is used in the next lesson.

Driving Lesson 47 - Replacing Text

Park and Read

Text can be searched for and replaced automatically.

Manoeuvres

1. Select cell **A1** in the **Hotel** workbook and click the **Find & Select** button in the **Editing** group. Select **Replace**.

2. In the **Find what** box, enter **room** and in **Replace with**, enter **chamber**.

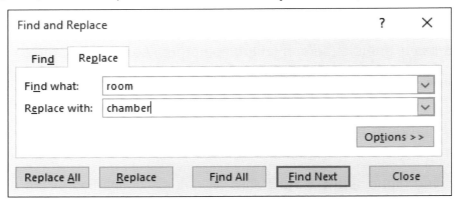

3. Click on **Find Next**. The first occurrence of **room** is highlighted. It may be necessary to move the **Find and Replace** dialog box so that the selected cell can be seen.

4. Click on **Replace** to change it to **chamber**. Continue clicking **Replace** to change all of the instances of room to chamber. When all are replaced a message dialog box is displayed.

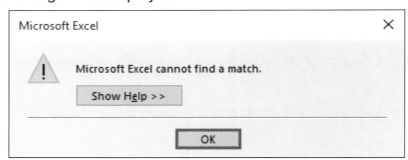

5. Click **OK**.

6. In the **Find what** box enter **chamber** and in **Replace with** enter **Bedroom**. This time click **Replace All**.

7. All occurrences of **chamber** have now been replaced with **Bedroom**. Click **OK** and then close the **Find and Replace** dialog box.

8. Close the workbook <u>without</u> saving.

Driving Lesson 48 - Sorting

▣ Park and Read

In a list, rows can be arranged in a specific order. The **Sort A to Z** button, $\boxed{^A_Z{\downarrow}~\text{Sort A to Z}}$, and the **Sort Z to A** button, $\boxed{^Z_A{\downarrow}~\text{Sort Z to A}}$, are used to sort text. The button text changes to **Sort Smallest to Largest** and **Sort Largest to Smallest** when sorting numbers. The rows are sorted automatically on the column containing the active cell.

⬏ Manoeuvres

1. Start a new workbook.

2. Enter a column of 8 names (surnames or first names) starting in cell **B3**.

3. To sort the names into ascending alphabetic order, first click in an occupied cell in column **B**.

4. From the **Home** tab, select **Sort & Filter** in the **Editing** group and then click **Sort A to Z**, $\boxed{^A_Z{\downarrow}~\text{Sort A to Z}}$. Notice the effect.

5. With the active cell still in column **B**, click **Sort & Filter** again but select **Sort Z to A**, $\boxed{^Z_A{\downarrow}~\text{Sort Z to A}}$. The names are sorted into descending order.

6. Add ages (in years) in column **C** adjacent to the names.

7. To sort the ages list into ascending order, first click in an occupied cell in column **C**.

8. Click **Sort & Filter** and select **Sort Smallest to Largest**. The ages are sorted in ascending order with the names in column **B** kept with correct ages.

ⓘ *You can also find these sorting commands in the **Sort & Filter** group on the* **Data** *tab.*

9. Now try sorting the ages into descending order.

ⓘ *More complicated sorting can be carried out by clicking the **Sort** button on the* **Data** *tab. This displays a dialog box with more sorting options.*

10. Close the workbook <u>without</u> saving.

Driving Lesson 49 - Revision

▣ Park and Read

At the end of every section you get the chance to complete one or more revision exercises to develop your skills and prepare you for your ECDL certification test. You should aim to complete the following steps without referring back to the previous lessons.

⬏ Manoeuvres

1. Open the workbook **Home Finances**.

2. Examine your finances to decide whether you can afford to buy a new camera, costing £90, for a holiday in August. Go to cell **N16** and look at your total savings for the end of the year. They are estimated to be less than you need to buy the camera, so drastic action is needed if you do not want to owe money at the end of the year.

3. From the beginning of January you decide to stop using your car and save petrol by cycling to work for three months. Select the range of cells for **Petrol** expenses from **Jan** through to **Mar**. As you feel extremely health conscious you decide to extend your cycling through to July; use the <**Shift**> key to extend the range to **Jul** and clear the cell contents.

4. Check **N16**. How much savings do you now have?

5. This good news is short lived as you realise that you do not own a bike and will have to continue to use the car. Click the **Undo** button to put the figures for your petrol back into the worksheet.

6. You now decide to limit your **Leisure** expenses to a maximum of £50 per month from **Jan** through to **Jul**. Type **50** in **Jan Leisure** (cell **B7**) and use the fill handle to copy this through to **Jul**.

⊿	A	B	C	D	E	F	G	H	I
1	*House Finance*	Jan	Feb	Mar	Apr	May	Jun	Jul	Aug
2	Pay	415	415	415	415	415	415	415	415
3	Other Income	0	0	0	0	0	0	0	0
4	Total Income	415	415	415	415	415	415	415	415
5	Rent	80	80	80	80	80	80	80	90
6	Holidays	0	0	0	50	0	0	0	210
7	Leisure	50	50	50	50	50	50	50	187
8	Electricity	49	0	0	43	0	0	29	0
9	Gas	46	0	0	51	0	0	32	0
10	Telephone	0	37	0	0	35	0	0	36

7. Check **N16**, how much have you now saved?

8. You intend to purchase the camera in July so add **90** to the figure already in **Others** for July (increasing it to **181**).

9. How much will you have in your savings by the end of the year now?

10. Close the workbook <u>without</u> saving.

Driving Lesson 50 - Revision

Manoeuvres

1. Create a blank spreadsheet. Enter **February** in **B2**, **Week 1** in **C3** and **Mon** in **B4**. Use the **Fill Handle** to produce the following sheet.

	A	B	C	D	E	F	G
1							
2		February					
3			Week1	Week2	Week3	Week4	Week5
4		Mon					
5		Tue					
6		Wed					
7		Thu					
8		Fri					
9		Sat					
10		Sun					

2. The first day of **February 2012** was a **Wednesday**. Type **01/02/12** into cell **C6**. By default, dates are displayed in the format, **01/02/2012**. Use the **Fill Handle** to drag **C6** to **C10**.

3. Enter **06/02/12** in cell **D4**, **13/02/12** in cell **E4**, **20/02/12** in cell **F4 and 27/02/12** in cell **G4**.

4. Fill the blank days of the week using the **Fill Handle** a column at a time. On which weekday was the last day of **Feb** and was **2012** a leap year?

5. In cell **B13** type **Year**. In cell **B14** type the year you were born, e.g. **1983**.

6. Use the **<Ctrl>** key to fill the cells below **B14** by dragging down the column until the series of dates reaches the present year.

7. In cell **C13** type **Age** and in cell **C14** type **0**, as you were born in that year.

8. Fill the column down increasing the series by **1** each time until you reach the current year. You should now see how old you will be this year.

9. In cell **D13** type **Days Old**. In cell **D14** type **0** and in **D15** type **365**. Highlight the two numbers and use the **Fill Handle** to fill down the column. Remember that this is an approximate figure as no account is taken for leap years.

10. Continue to increase the series in column **C** until **65**. Increase column **B** and **D** also to match column **C**. How many days old will you be or were you when **65** years old?

11. Close the workbook <u>without</u> saving.

Sample answers can be found at the back of the guide.

*Now complete the **Record of Achievement Matrix** at the back of the guide. You should only move on when confident with the topics and features described in this section.*

Section 7
Printing

By the end of this section you should be able to:

Print a Worksheet and Workbook

Use Print Preview

Change the Page Setup

Add Headers and Footers

Use Print Titles

Display and Print Formulas

Print Specified Areas of a Worksheet

Work through the **Driving Lessons** in this section to gain an understanding of the above features.

For each **Driving Lesson**, read all of the **Park and Read** instructions and then perform the numbered steps of the **Manoeuvres**. Complete the **Revision** exercise(s) at the end of the section to test your knowledge.

Driving Lesson 51 - Printing

🄿 Park and Read

Worksheets can be printed to give a hard copy. It is possible to decide what to print: the sheet, the pages and the number of copies.

☞ Manoeuvres

1. Open the workbook **Company** and notice it contains two sheets. The **Actual** sheet is small and fits easily on one piece of A4 paper.

2. Click the **File** tab and select **Print** (or use the key press <**Ctrl P**>) to display the **Print** options screen. The left-hand side controls what is printed. The right-hand side shows a useful *preview* of what will print.

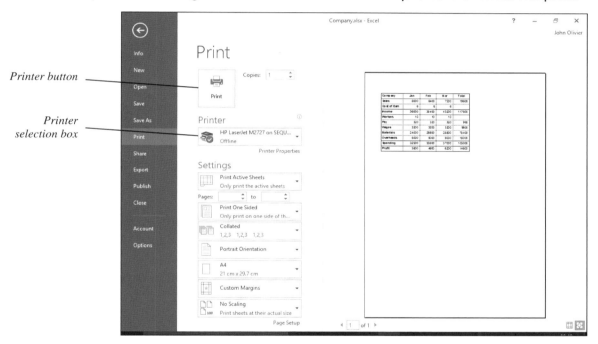

3. Examine the options on the left. The default settings are to print **1** copy of the **Active sheet** on **A4** sized paper. You can select a printer from those available by clicking the printer selection box.

4. Click the large **Print** button to print one copy of the worksheet on your default printer (or press <**Esc**> to return without printing).

5. All the worksheets in a workbook can be printed. Click the **File** tab and then **Print** again. Click **Print Active Sheets** under **Settings** and select **Print Entire Workbook**.

6. Click the **Print** button to print the entire workbook on your default printer (or press <**Esc**> to return without printing). Two sheets are printed.

7. Close the workbook <u>without</u> saving.

Driving Lesson 52 - Print Preview

▣ Park and Read

In *Excel 2016* print preview is integrated into the **Print** options screen. The preview is shown on the right. The preview shows the layout of the worksheet on the page(s). **Page Setup** can be activated from here by clicking the **Page Setup** link. This link is used to perform tasks that are not available from the **Print** options screen, e.g. controlling **Headers and Footers**.

⬏ Manoeuvres

1. Open the workbook **Exam Results**. Click the **File** tab and then click the **Print** option.

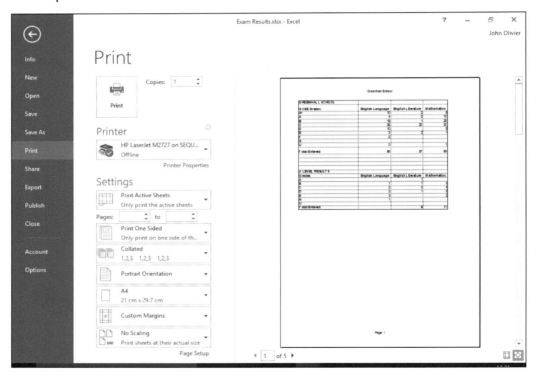

2. The preview on the right shows how the worksheet will look when printed. The worksheet covers five pages.

3. At the bottom of the preview are page navigation buttons, ◀ 1 of 5 ▶. Click the right arrow, **Next Page**, to view the second page.

4. Use the **Next Page** and **Previous Page** arrows to view the rest of the pages in this 5-page workbook. Return to **Page 1**.

ℹ *The scroll bar can also be used to display the pages of a multi-page worksheet.*

5. Leave the workbook open for the next lesson.

Driving Lesson 53 - Page Setup

Park and Read

Page Setup is used to change the way a worksheet is printed. Pages can be printed in either **Portrait** or **Landscape** or can be scaled to fit on a number of pages. However, many of these features can now be controlled within the **Print** options screen under **Settings**.

Manoeuvres

1. The workbook **Exam Results** should still be open with the **Print** screen displayed. Note that there are **5** pages.

2. The page settings are controlled via the **Settings** options listed on the left.

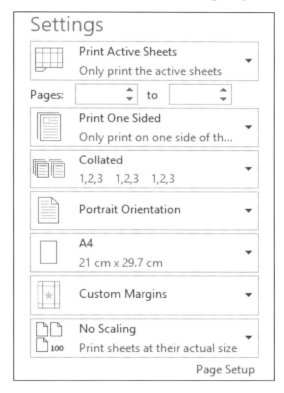

3. Click the **Portrait Orientation** option and select **Landscape Orientation**.

4. There are now three pages, notice that **Landscape** is where the largest edge of the paper is across the top.

5. Use the **Next Page** and **Previous Page** arrows to view all the pages.

6. To fit the worksheet to a set number of pages the **Scaling** option is used. Click the **No Scaling** option and select the **Fit Sheet on One Page** option. The worksheet will be fitted on a single page. It may be a little difficult to read.

Driving Lesson 53 - Continued

 *The **Scaling** option can be set to any number of required pages, e.g. **1** wide by **3** tall. The worksheet will be scaled to fit within the 3 pages. It may occupy less pages but not more. This is achieved by selecting **Custom Scaling Options** and then entering the required pages to the right of **Fit to**.*

7.   Click the **Fit Sheet on One Page** option and select **No Scaling** to return the worksheet to its previous setting of 3 pages.

8.   The default **Paper size** is **A4**, but this can be changed if working with different sized paper. Click the **A4** option.

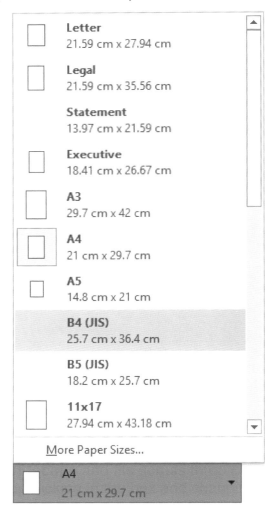

*The actual **Paper size** options available will depend on the model of printer in use.*

9.   Examine the list and then select **A5**. The worksheet is now on 10 pages.

10. Change the paper size back to **A4**.

11. Leave the workbook open for the next lesson.

Driving Lesson 54 - Margins

▣ Park and Read

Margins can be reduced or enlarged to give more or less white space around a worksheet. Margins are normally reduced to allow more of a worksheet to fit on each piece of paper.

⌒ Manoeuvres

1. Using the workbook **Exam Results**, in the **Print** options, select **Custom Margins**.

Normal
Top: 1.91 cm   Bottom: 1.91 cm
Left: 1.78 cm   Right: 1.78 cm
Header: 0.76 cm   Footer: 0.76 cm

Wide
Top: 2.54 cm   Bottom: 2.54 cm
Left: 2.54 cm   Right: 2.54 cm
Header: 1.27 cm   Footer: 1.27 cm

Narrow
Top: 1.91 cm   Bottom: 1.91 cm
Left: 0.64 cm   Right: 0.64 cm
Header: 0.76 cm   Footer: 0.76 cm

★ **Custom Margins**

Custom Margins...

2. This displays only limited options, **Normal**, **Wide** and **Narrow**. For more control, click the **Custom Margins** text at the bottom of the list.

3. The **Page Setup** dialog box is displayed. To change **Margin** settings (values are in centimetres), either type in the values or use ⬆⬇ to increase or decrease the values within the **Top**, **Bottom**, **Left** and **Right** boxes. The worksheet is **Landscape** and fits across three pages; reduce the **Left** margin down to **0.4** by clicking in the box and changing the amount.

4. Change the **Right** margin down to **0.4** by clicking three times on the down spinner (the down triangle).

5. Clicking in the **Center on page** boxes centres the worksheet horizontally and/or vertically. Check both the **Horizontally** and **Vertically** options. Click **OK** to accept the changes. There are now only two pages with the worksheet centred on each page.

6. Close **Exam Results** and click **Don't Save** to close <u>without</u> saving.

Driving Lesson 55 - Printing a Selection

▣ Park and Read

It is possible to print a small part of a worksheet only; a selected range for example. You might want to do this when only a small area of the worksheet is relevant for your intended audience.

⌒↱ Manoeuvres

1. Open the workbook **Hotel**.

2. Select the range **A3:E17** (the first four months of receipts).

3. Click the **File** tab and then **Print** (or use the key press <**Ctrl P**>) to display the **Print** options screen.

ℹ *Locate the **Pages** boxes under **Print Active Sheets**. When printing a multi-page worksheet you have the option to print selected pages only. Enter the range of pages to print here (start to end). For example, entering **2** to **3** would only print pages **2** and **3**.*

4. Click **Print Active Sheets** and select **Print Selection**.

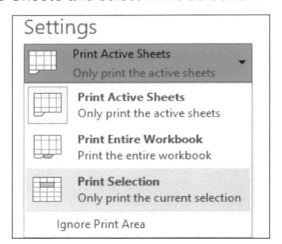

5. Notice the print preview. Only the selected cells (**A3:E17**) will now be printed.

ℹ *Locate the **Copies** button to the right of the **Print** button. This can be used to increase the number of copies of a print. For now, leave this as **1**.*

6. Click the **Print** button to print the selection on your default printer (or press <**Esc**> to return without printing).

7. Close the workbook <u>without</u> saving.

Driving Lesson 56 - Headers and Footers

▣ Park and Read

Headers and **Footers** are lines of text which appear at the top and bottom of every printed page. They can contain text or **field codes** in the three areas: **Left section**, **Center section** and **Right section**.

ℹ *Field codes are text placeholders that Excel automatically updates when you print a worksheet. They are useful for dates, times and page numbers that constantly change.*

↷ Manoeuvres

1. Open the workbook **League**. This is a workbook that contains information about various hockey leagues.

2. Display the **Insert** tab. From the **Text** group, click the **Header & Footer** button. This displays the **Header** on the worksheet and the **Design** tab within **Header & Footer Tools**. The view is called **Page Layout**.

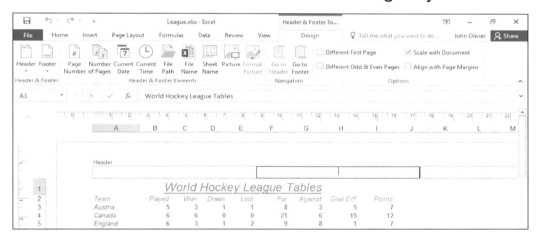

3. Examine the **Design** tab to see the available tools when dealing with **Headers and Footers**.

4. Text can be entered by typing in any of the sections; left, centre or right. The cursor is currently placed in the **Center section** of the header. Type the title **World Hockey Tables**.

5. Place the cursor in the **Right section** and type **Provisional**.

6. Scroll down the worksheet to see the header on both pages.

ℹ *When adding a title choose between using a cell on the worksheet or a **Header**.*

7. Click on the **Header** and edit the centre text to **World Hockey League Tables**. Delete the text in the right section to remove it.

Driving Lesson 56 - Continued

8.　The title on row 1 is no longer needed. Click on cell **A1** and press <**Delete**> to remove the cell's contents.

9.　Click in the header again. Display the **Design** tab and click the **Go to Footer** button in the **Navigation** group. The footer is shown.

10.　Click in the **Left section** and then click the **Current Date** button. This places the field code **&[Date]** in the box. This code displays the current date.

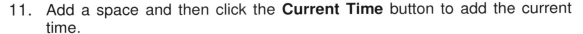

11.　Add a space and then click the **Current Time** button to add the current time.

&[Date] &[Time]

Footer

12.　Click in the **Center section**. Notice the left section now displays the codes as text, e.g. 07/10/2015 11:52.

13.　Type **Page** followed by a space and then click the **Page number** button. *Excel* places the field code **&[Page]** in the box.

14.　Click in the **Right section** and click the **Sheet Name** button.

15.　Add a space and then click the **File Name** button. The field codes are **&[Tab]** and **&[File]**. These help identify the printout by displaying the sheet and book names.

16.　Scroll the worksheet to check each part of the **Footer**. Check both pages.

i　*To delete a field in a **Header/Footer**, select the field code and press <**Delete**>.*

17.　The worksheet has two pages in **Landscape** view. Display the **Page Layout** tab, click the **Orientation** button and select **Portrait**.

18.　To change the view back to normal display the **View** tab and click the **Normal** button.

i　*Click the **Page Layout** button on the **View** tab to show the headers and footers on the worksheet.*

19.　Preview the worksheet and notice the changes. The header and footer text appears.

i　*You can add field codes to both the header and footer.*

20.　Save the workbook as **League2** and close it.

i　*Headers and footers can also be created and edited using the **Header/Footer** tab within the **Page Setup** dialog box.*

Driving Lesson 57 - Print Titles

Park and Read

Rows and columns of the worksheet may be specified as titles, and these can be displayed on each printed page.

Manoeuvres

1. Open the workbook **Survey**.

2. Display the **Page Layout** tab and click the **Print Titles** button.

3. The **Page Setup** dialog box showing the **Sheet** tab is displayed.

4. Click in the **Rows to repeat at top** box and then click the **Collapse** button, ▦, to the right of the box.

5. Click and drag to select rows **1** to **5** on the worksheet (the collapsed dialog box may have to be moved to do this).

6. Click the **Expand** button, ▦, to expand the dialog box again.

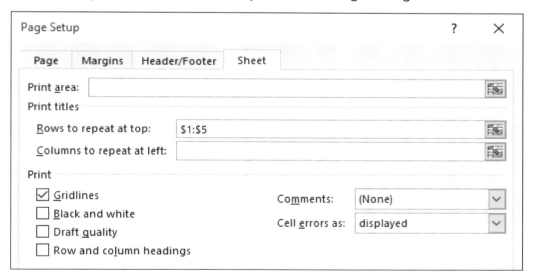

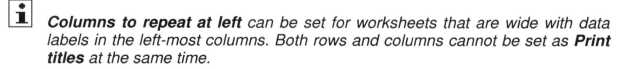

*Columns to repeat at left can be set for worksheets that are wide with data labels in the left-most columns. Both rows and columns cannot be set as **Print titles** at the same time.*

7. Click **OK**.

8. Click the **File** tab and then **Print**. Use the **Next Page** arrow to see the other pages. Notice that the first five rows of the worksheet are repeated on every page.

9. Close the workbook <u>without</u> saving.

Driving Lesson 58 - Displaying & Printing Formulas

▣ Park and Read

Instead of formula results, the actual formulas themselves can be displayed on screen and then printed. This is useful when checking that formulas are correct.

☞ Manoeuvres

1. Open the workbook **Formulas** which contains some simple calculations.

2. Type **6** in cell **B4** and press <**Enter**>. Is the answer correct in **B6**? Click on cell **B6**. Check the **Formula Bar** for the formula.

3. To display all the formulas on the screen, display the **Formulas** tab and, in the **Formula Auditing** group, click the **Show Formulas** button, 🔲. The formulas are now shown.

i *Alternatively, and much more quickly, it is possible to switch between formulas and their results by pressing <Ctrl `>, i.e. Ctrl and the key to the left of 1.*

4. Switch to the results and then switch back to the formulas using the quick key press method.

5. There is a problem with cell **D6**, it contains the number **10**. Enter the formula to multiply the two numbers **=d4*d5**.

6. If the formulas are to be printed, it is normal to display the row and column headings and the gridlines with the formulas so they can be checked. Display the **Page Layout** tab and then check **Print** under **Gridlines** and **Print** under **Headings** (in the **Sheet Options** group).

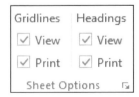

7. Click the **File** tab and select **Print**. Notice the print preview on the right – the formulas, gridlines and column/row headings are all shown.

8. Press <**Esc**> to return to the worksheet. On the **Page Layout** tab uncheck **Print** under **Gridlines** and **Print** under **Headings** to stop the **Headings** and **Gridlines** from being printed.

9. Click the **Show Formulas** button on the **Formulas** tab to remove the displayed formulas.

10. Close the workbook <u>without</u> saving.

Driving Lesson 59 - Revision

▣ Park and Read

At the end of every section you get the chance to complete one or more revision exercises to develop your skills and prepare you for your ECDL certification test. You should aim to complete the following steps without referring back to the previous lessons.

↷ Manoeuvres

1. Open the workbook **Oscars**.

2. Add a centred header **Oscar Winners** and insert page numbering in the right section of the footer.

3. Change the page orientation to **Landscape**.

4. Change the top and bottom, margins to **2.0**.

5. Change the left and right margins to **0.4**.

6. Select and print the last 10 Oscar winning films only.

7. Change the **Print Titles** to repeat row 1 on all the pages.

8. Print a copy of the entire worksheet.

9. Close the workbook <u>without</u> saving.

Driving Lesson 60 - Revision

Manoeuvres

1. Open the workbook **Hotel**.

2. Alter the page settings for printing to the following:

   Header -   Change to **Company Finances** (centred)

   Footer -   Remove the word **Page** to leave just the page number

   Margins -   **Top** and **Bottom** to **2cm** and **Left** and **Right** to **1cm**

3. Print out **Page 2** only.

4. Using **Page Titles**, select to repeat **Column A**.

5. Select the range **F3:J14** and print the selection.

6. Close the workbook <u>without</u> saving.

7. Open the workbook **Company**. This is a small workbook containing two worksheets, **Actual** and **Forecast**.

8. The worksheets are very similar and it is difficult to identify which is which from the printed copies. Add a centred **Sheet Name** code to each of the worksheets in the footer.

9. Print a copy of the entire workbook.

10. Close the **Company** workbook <u>without</u> saving.

 *Now complete the **Record of Achievement Matrix** at the back of the guide. You should only move on when confident with the topics and features described in this section.*

Section 8
Formatting

By the end of this section you should be able to:

Format Numbers, Dates and Percentages

Change Cell Alignment and Rotate Text

Add Borders and Colour

Change Row Height and Column Width

Insert and Delete Rows and Columns

Use Freeze and Zoom

Use the Format Painter

Work through the **Driving Lessons** in this section to gain an understanding of the above features.

For each **Driving Lesson**, read all of the **Park and Read** instructions and then perform the numbered steps of the **Manoeuvres**. Complete the **Revision** exercise(s) at the end of the section to test your knowledge.

Driving Lesson 61 - Formatting

Park and Read

To **Format** a worksheet is to change the way cells look in order to improve their overall appearance. The **Home** tab can be used to achieve the full range of formatting.

Formatting can change the style, size, colour, alignment and number format of text and numbers, as well as the border style, colour and pattern of cells.

Manoeuvres

1. Open the workbook **Climate**.

2. Display the **Home** tab and click **Format** in the **Cells** group. Select **Format Cells**. The cells to be formatted would normally be selected before using this command, but it is used here to show the variety of features that are available.

3. The **Format Cells** dialog box is displayed. This is a dialog box with six tabs.

4. The **Number** tab is first. If this is not currently displayed, click it now. This tab controls the way numbers are shown, including dates and times.

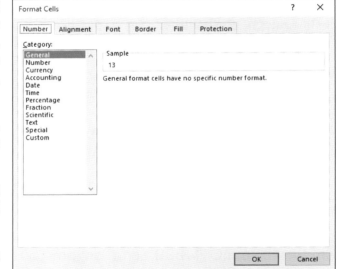

5. Click the **Alignment** tab. This positions information in cells.

6. Click **Font**. This changes the text style, size and other formatting features.

7. Click **Border**. This controls the lines around the cells.

8. Click **Fill**. This controls background cell colour.

9. Click **Protection**. This is part of a system to stop information being lost.

*Most of the formatting features described here are also available using buttons visible on the **Ribbon**, as you will learn in the following lessons.*

10. Click **Cancel** to close the **Format Cells** dialog box.

11. Leave the workbook open for the next lesson.

Driving Lesson 62 - Bold, Underline & Italic

▣ Park and Read

The easiest way to make a cell stand out is to make it **Bold**. This works well with titles.

Underline is a line under the cell contents (not a cell border).

Italic gives you leaning text.

↱ Manoeuvres

1. Using the workbook **Climate**, select the cells **B2:J2**.

2. To make this range of cells **Bold**, click the **Bold** button, ▢ B , in the **Font** group.

ℹ *The button is displayed with a different background to show the feature is active. This applies to all the formatting buttons.*

3. Select cells **A2:A18** and click once on the following buttons: **Italic**, ▢ I , and **Underline**, ▢ U ▾ .

4. Click anywhere on the worksheet to remove the highlighted selection and see the results. The underlining of a column of labels is not very effective.

5. Select cells **A2:A18** again and click the **Underline** button, ▢ U ▾ , to turn off the underlining. Click anywhere on the worksheet to remove the highlighted section.

6. There are quick key presses for bold, italic and underline. Click on cell **A2**. Press <**Ctrl B**> to add **Bold**, and to add **Underline**, press <**Ctrl U**>. The key press for **Italic** is <**Ctrl I**>, but this cell already has **Italic** added.

7. The same keys turn off the formatting. Press <**Ctrl I**> and <**Ctrl U**> to turn off italic and underline for cell **A2**.

ℹ *The **Font** tab within the **Format Cells** dialog box could have been used to apply this formatting but the buttons and key presses shown here are quicker.*

ℹ *The **Underline** button has a drop-down arrow with a **Double Underline** option. After applying a double underline the button changes to* ▢ D ▾

8. To double underline the contents of cell **A2**, click the drop-down arrow on the **Underline** button in the **Font** group and select **Double Underline**.

9. Leave the workbook open for the next lesson.

Driving Lesson 63 - Fonts & Font Size

▣ Park and Read

A **Font** is a type or style of print. Examples of fonts are Arial, Times New Roman, Modern, *Script*, etc. The default font and font size is **Calibri 11**. **Font Size** is measured in points – more points means a larger size.

⟳ Manoeuvres

1. Using the workbook **Climate**, make sure cell **A2** is selected. To change the font for this cell, a selection can be made using the **Font** drop-down button in the **Font** group. As the mouse pointer moves over each font in the list the results are previewed on the worksheet.

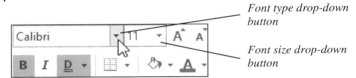

Font type drop-down button

Font size drop-down button

2. Change the font to **Arial**.

3. Highlight the range **B2:J2** and change the font to **Times New Roman**.

4. To make fonts bigger you can change their size. Select cell **A2** and click the drop-down button on the **Font Size** box.

5. Select **14** (clicking on the **11** and typing **14** also works – this is especially useful when a size is not displayed in the list).

ℹ️ *If row height has not been manually changed then an increase in font size automatically increases row height to display the text correctly.*

6. Select cells **B2:J2** and change the font size to **12**.

7. The formatting of a cell can be copied to other cell(s) using the **Format Painter**. Click on cell **B2**, click the **Format Painter** button, 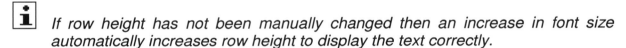, in the **Clipboard** group, then click and drag the range **B3:K4**. On release of the mouse button the format of cell **B2** is copied to the range **B3:K4**.

8. Check that the cells in the range **B3:K4** are **Times New Roman** font, size **12** and **bold**.

ℹ️ *To use the **Format Painter** button repeatedly, double click it to keep the feature turned on. When finished, press <**Esc**> to turn it off.*

9. Leave the workbook open for the next lesson.

ℹ️ *These changes can be made using the **Format Cells** dialog box.*

Driving Lesson 64 - Format Number

▣ Park and Read

Numbers can be displayed in various styles, with decimal places, including a £ sign, % signs, with or without a separator to indicate thousands, etc.

⌐ Manoeuvres

1.   Use the workbook **Climate** and select the range **B5:K16**.

2.   Click the drop-down arrow, ▾, on **Number Format**, General ▾, in the **Number** group.

3.   Select **More Number Formats** from the options displayed. The **Format Cells** dialog box appears.

4.   On the **Number** tab, select **Number** under **Category** on the left.

5.   Check that the number of **Decimal places** is set to **2**.

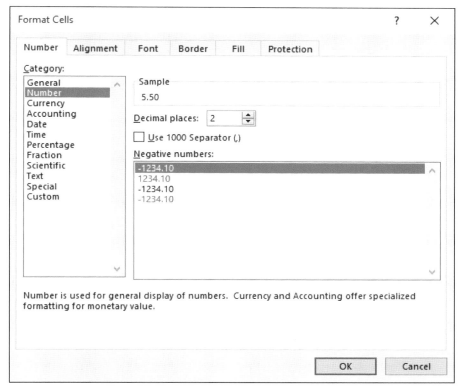

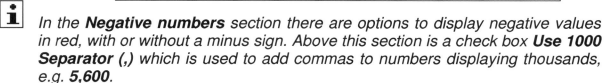

*In the **Negative numbers** section there are options to display negative values in red, with or without a minus sign. Above this section is a check box **Use 1000 Separator (,)** which is used to add commas to numbers displaying thousands, e.g. **5,600**.*

6.   Click **OK** to apply the chosen formats. All the numbers in the range are now formatted to two decimal places.

Driving Lesson 64 - Continued

7. There are also buttons in the **Number** group to **Increase Decimal**, 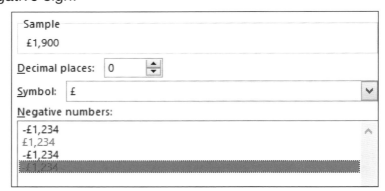, and **Decrease Decimal**, places (by one place for each click). With the cells **B5:K16** still selected, click the **Decrease Decimal** button, . The numbers are displayed to one decimal place.

> *After applying number formats, cells may display **#######**. This means that the number is too big for the cell. The data is not lost but the column must be widened. This is covered in lesson 67.*

8. Close the workbook <u>without</u> saving.

9. Open the workbook **Budget**. This workbook contains cells with large numbers and currency values.

10. Highlight the range **B7:N7**. To format this range as numbers with comma separators and no decimal places, display the **Format Cells** dialog box and, from the **Number** tab, click **Number** in the **Category** list. Change the **Decimal places** to **0** and check **Use 1000 Separator (,)**. Click **OK**.

11. The tax rates are shown as decimals and would be better shown as percentages. Highlight the range **B12:M12** and click the **%** button, . This is quicker than using the **Format Cells** dialog box.

12. The total rows are to be formatted as currency. Highlight the range **B4:N4** and, while holding down the <**Ctrl**> key, select the ranges **B10:N10** and **B14:N14**. The three separate ranges are now highlighted. Display the **Format Cells** dialog box and click **Currency** in the **Category** list. Change the **Decimal places** to **0**, add the **£** sign from the **Symbol** drop-down list and, under **Negative numbers**, select to display negative numbers in red with a negative sign.

13. Click **OK**.

14. Format the ranges **B2:N2**, **B8:N9**, **B11:N11** and **B13:N13** as numbers, with no decimal places but with comma separators for thousands.

15. Save the workbook as **Budget2** and close it.

Driving Lesson 65 - Dates

Park and Read

Date and **Time** are stored as numbers. The **Date** is a number representing the number of days since 1 January 1900. The **Time** is a decimal, as part of a day.

Both the **Date** and **Time** can be displayed in various formats including numbers and text.

Manoeuvres

1. Start a new workbook.

2. In cell **B2** enter your birthday, in the form of **24/2/88**. Press <**Enter**>.

3. Make **B2** the active cell again.

4. Display the **Format Cells** dialog box and choose the **Number** tab.

5. Select **Date** from the **Category** section and select each format from within **Type**. A preview is shown in the **Sample** box.

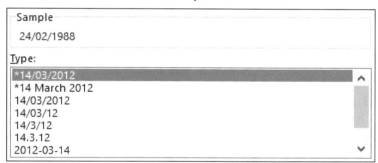

6. Select **14 March 2012** format. Click **OK**.

Selections within **Regional Settings** within the **Control Panel** affect the display of the date.

7. Click in cell **B4** and enter today's date by pressing <**Ctrl ;**>. This is the quick key press for the current date, it is entered as text. Press <**Enter**> to complete the entry.

8. Repeat the above steps to display today's date in a different format.

9. Click in cell **B6** and enter the current time by pressing <**Ctrl Shift ;**> Press <**Enter**>.

10. Click in cell **B6**. To change the format of the time, display the **Format Cells** dialog box and select the **Number** tab. Under **Time** all the **Types** include seconds. Select the **Category** as **Custom** and select the **Type** as **h:mm AM/PM**. Click **OK** and notice the effect.

11. Close the workbook <u>without</u> saving.

Driving Lesson 66 - Alignment

▣ Park and Read

Alignment is the positioning of text in a cell relative to its edges. By default labels (text) are aligned to the left and numbers to the right.

⟲ Manoeuvres

1.   Open the workbook **House**.

2.   Select the range **B3:N3**. To horizontally align these titles differently there are 3 buttons on the **Home** tab **Alignment** group: **Align Left**, ▤ (the default setting), **Center**, ▤ and **Align Right**, ▤.

3.   Click the **Center** button, ▤, and the labels are centred. Click the **Align Right** button, ▤, and the labels are moved to the right.

4.   Click on cell **A1**. There are also buttons for vertical alignment. They are **Top Align**, ▤, **Middle Align**, ▤, and **Bottom Align**, ▤ (the default setting). Click the **Middle Align** button. The text is in the centre of the cell, vertically.

5.   The title is in cell **A1**. To centre it across the width of the worksheet, highlight the range **A1:N1** and click the **Merge & Center** button, ▤▾, in the **Alignment** group. The cells are merged, with the title in the centre.

6.   The **Merge & Center** button has a drop-down for other options. With the merged cell selected, click the **Merge & Center** drop-down.

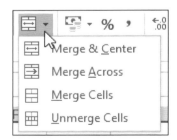

7.   The options are displayed. This controls how the cells are merged.

8.   Select **Unmerge Cells**. The cells are unmerged. Left align cell **A1**.

ℹ️ *Cells already merged can be unmerged by clicking the button without using the drop-down list.*

9.   Rename the sheet as **House Finance**.

10. Insert a new worksheet.

Driving Lesson 66 - Continued

11. On the new **Sheet1**, create the following (note that the text **Telephone Extension** is all entered in cell **B3**; it flows into **C3**):

	A	B	C	D
1				
2				
3	Names	Telephone Extension		
4	John	356		
5	Asif	871		
6	Suzanne	780		
7	Mary	247		
8	Hardeep	163		
9				

12. Select the range **A3:B8** and change the **Font Size** to **9pt**.

13. When the label across the top of a column is too long for the information below, the text can be wrapped within the cell. Click on cell **B3** and click the **Wrap Text** button, [icon], in the **Alignment** group.

> *Text wrap can be applied to a range of cells - just select the range first.*

14. The text in **B3** is wrapped within the cell and row height is increased automatically. Column **C** can now be used normally.

	A	B	C
1			
2			
3	Names	Telephone Extension	
4	John	356	
5	Asif	871	
6	Suzanne	780	
7	Mary	247	
8	Hardeep	163	
9			

> *The row height is only adjusted automatically if it has not been adjusted manually. Row height and column width are covered in the next lessons.*

15. Save the workbook as **House2** and then close it.

Driving Lesson 67 - Changing Column Width

▣ Park and Read

Column Width is the horizontal space that a column occupies. It is measured in units.

⌒ Manoeuvres

1. Open the workbook **Growth**. Enter **Word Population Statistics** in **A1** and **2015** in **B1**.

2. The text in cell **A1** been chopped off because it extends beyond the cell boundary (and **B1** is not empty). Column **A** needs to be widened.

3. Position the mouse pointer in the **Column Headings** at the join between columns **A** and **B**. The mouse pointer changes to ✛.

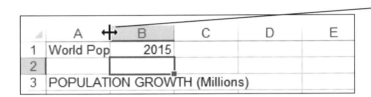

Click and drag to change the width of column A

4. Clicking and dragging to the left or right alters the width of the column to the left of the pointer (take care when dragging left as a width of **0** results in the column being hidden). As the pointer moves, the current column width measurement is displayed in units and pixels. Drag to the right to widen column **A** until it is **25.00** units wide.

5. To widen a column to fit to the largest entry, place the mouse pointer between **A** and **B** in the column heading as before and **double click**.

6. The column on the left is automatically adjusted to the widest entry in that column. This is **POPULATION GROWTH (Millions)**, cell **A3**.

ℹ *More than one column can be adjusted at the same time. To do this, select them in the **Column Headings** and adjust one – the others will change also.*

7. Click on **C** and drag across to **D** to select two columns.

8. Change either **C** or **D** to a width of **12** units. Both column widths are adjusted.

9. Leave the workbook open for the next lesson.

ℹ *There is also a menu option to change **Column Width**. Click the **Format** button in the **Cells** group and select **Column Width**. A number is then entered into the dialog box. Click **OK** to adjust the width.*

Driving Lesson 68 - Changing Row Height

Park and Read

Row Heights are increased to create more space between rows of data, making it easier to read the worksheet, or decreased to fit more data on a page.

Row heights are changed in the same way as changing column widths, except the adjust cursor is between two rows and it is the row above that is altered.

Manoeuvres

1. Using the workbook **Growth**, point in the **Row Border**, at the division between rows **4** and **5**. The mouse pointer changes to ✚.

2. The height of each row is **12.75** units. Clicking and dragging up or down now alters the height of the row above (take care when dragging up as a row can be hidden - **0** height). Carefully drag down to make the height of row **4** about **20**.

3. Select rows **5** to **12** by dragging in the **Row Border**. Adjust any row by dragging the adjust cursor down until **Height 18.00 (24 pixels)** is displayed.

4. Click on any cell to deselect the rows.

5. Place the cursor between the **6** and **7** in the row border, to display the adjust cursor.

4	REGION		1975	1990
5	Asia		478	495
6	Africa		323	448
7	North America		212	265
8	South America		254	289

6. Double clicking the adjust cursor between the rows automatically adjusts the row above to the highest entry on that row. Double click and the row height is adjusted to the height of the text on row 6.

Double clicking, with the cursor at the division between the rows, is used after increasing the font size.

7. Click the **Undo** button to return row **6** to its previous height.

8. Leave the workbook open for the next lesson.

*There is also a menu option to change **Row Height**. Click the **Format** button in the **Cells** group and select **Row Height**. A specific height can then be entered into the dialog box. Click **OK** to apply the new height setting.*

Driving Lesson 69 - Inserting Rows and Columns

🅿 Park and Read

Rows and columns can be inserted into a worksheet between existing rows and columns when items have been forgotten or when new data is to be added.

A problem arises if a worksheet is fully developed with formulas in place. Rows or columns inserted at either end of a range, i.e. the first or last items, will mean an adjustment of all the formulas. **Check all formulas after inserting rows or columns**.

⏎ Manoeuvres

1. Using the workbook **Growth**, let's insert a new column between **1975** and **1990** (columns **C** and **D**). Click on any cell in column **D** and, on the **Home** tab, click the **Insert** button's drop-down arrow (in the **Cells** group).

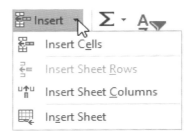

2. Select **Insert Sheet Columns**. A new column is inserted to the left of column **D**.

ℹ️ *New columns are inserted to the left of the active cell and new rows are inserted above it.*

3. Click **Undo** to reverse the action. A column can be inserted using another method. Right click the column heading **D** and select **Insert** from the shortcut menu. A column is inserted.

ℹ️ *Rows are inserted in much the same way.*

4. Multiple rows and columns can be inserted by selecting the required number of rows or columns on the heading bars first. For example, to insert 2 rows, click and drag on the **Row Headings** to select the row numbers **4** and **5** (two rows).

5. Click the **Insert** button. Two new rows are inserted as 4 and 5 above the selected rows.

6. Leave the workbook open for the next lesson.

Driving Lesson 70 - Deleting Rows and Columns

▣ Park and Read

Unwanted extra rows or columns can be deleted.

↱ Manoeuvres

1. Using the workbook **Growth**, let's delete **Column B**. Select column **B** by clicking in the column heading.

2. Click **Delete** in the **Cells** group. Column **B** is now deleted and columns to the right move left one.

3. To delete rows **4** and **5**, select the two rows, right click and select **Delete**. Rows 4 and 5 are deleted and the other rows move up to fill the space.

4. To remove row 2 by another method, right click in any cell on the row and select **Delete**.

5. Select the required option in the **Delete** dialog box, in this case, **Entire row**. Click on **OK** to delete the row.

6. Close the workbook <u>without</u> saving.

ⓘ *The results in cell formulas may be altered by deleting parts of the worksheet, resulting in errors indicated by **#REF** in the cells.*

Driving Lesson 71 - Adding Borders

▆ Park and Read

Borders are lines around the edges of cells. Border options are available to change the line style, colour and placement of border lines.

↱ Manoeuvres

1. Open the workbook **Rainfall**. One line has already been added under row **1**. This line needs to be thicker.

2. With cell **A1** selected, click the drop-down arrow next to the **Borders** button, ⬚ ▾ , in the **Font** group to display a drop-down list.

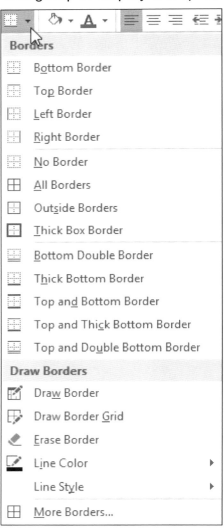

3. There are 13 border options and 5 drawing options, plus a **More Borders** option. Select **Thick Bottom Border**. A thick line is added under the selected cell. Click away from the cell to see the results.

Driving Lesson 71 - Continued

4. The last chosen option is displayed for future use on the **Borders** button. Highlight the range **B1:E1** and click the **Borders** <u>button</u> to apply the last chosen option, i.e. a thick bottom line.

5. More borders are available using the **More Borders** option at the bottom of the **Borders** menu. Highlight the range **A1:E13**, click the **Borders** drop-down and select **More Borders** to display the **Border** tab on the **Format Cells** dialog box.

6. Under **Presets**, click the **None** button to remove all borders in the currently selected range.

7. Lines are added to the range of selected cells by clicking the **Presets**, the **Border** buttons or the **Preview** diagram. To add a double line around the outside of the selected cells, click the last option in **Style** (the double line) and then click the **Outline** button under **Presets**.

8. If coloured lines are required, the colour must be selected before adding the lines. To add blue lines to the inside of the selected area, click the **Color** drop-down and select **blue**.

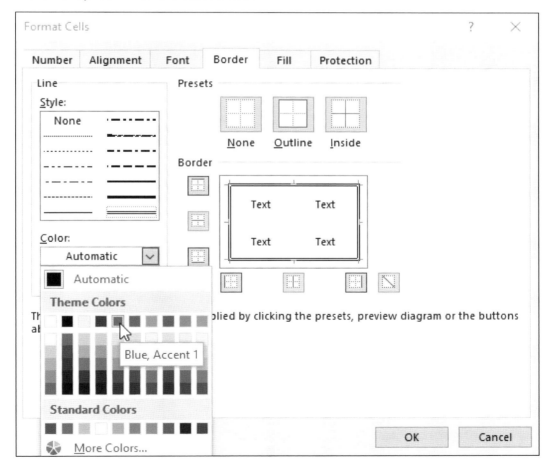

9. Then select the dotted line style option within the **Line Style** box and then click **Inside** under **Presets**. The **Preview** should look like below.

Driving Lesson 71 - Continued

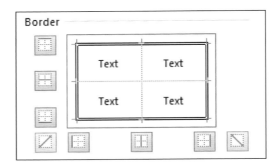

10. Click **OK** to add the lines.

11. When adding your own lines the gridlines on the worksheet can normally be turned off. Display the **Page Layout** tab and, in the **Sheet Options** group, uncheck **View** under **Gridlines**.

12. Click once anywhere on the worksheet to see the effect.

13. Next, let's improve the title row. select the range **A1:E1** and display the **Border** tab on the **Format Cells** dialog box again.

14. Select the double line in **Style** and click the bottom border button, ▦, under **Border**. This applies the selected style to the bottom of the range.

15. Select a single solid line (bottom left in the **Style** box), and click the vertical middle border button, ▦. Click **OK** and then click once anywhere on the worksheet to see the effect.

◢	A	B	C	D	E
1	RAINFALL(cms)	London	Mumbai	Adelaide	Tokyo
2	Jan	5.5	0.5	1.8	5.0
3	Feb	4.0	0.5	1.8	7.0
4	Mar	3.8	0.0	2.5	10.0
5	Apr	3.9	0.0	4.0	14.0
6	May	4.5	2.0	7.0	13.0
7	Jun	4.5	24.0	8.0	18.0
8	Jul	5.8	24.0	7.0	14.0
9	Aug	6.0	24.0	6.0	14.0
10	Sep	5.5	24.0	5.0	21.0
11	Oct	6.0	4.5	4.5	22.0
12	Nov	6.3	1.0	3.0	10.0
13	Dec	4.3	0.0	2.5	6.0

 *The **Format Painter**, 🖌, can be used for copying borders as well as text, alignment and colour to other cells.*

16. Close the workbook <u>without</u> saving.

Driving Lesson 72 - Adding Colour

⊞ Park and Read

Changing the colour of the text is similar to adding bold or italic - it highlights the text and it often looks better. *Excel* calls text colour, **Font Color**.

↱ Manoeuvres

1. Open the workbook **Format** and select the range **A2:A16**.

2. On the **Home** tab, click the **Font Color** button, ⬛. Click away from the range to see the colour change (**Red** is default).

3. Select the same range, **A2:A16**, and click the **Font Color** drop-down arrow to display the colour box.

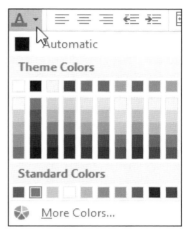

4. Select any **Blue** colour. Selecting a colour automatically closes the drop-down box and applies that colour to the text in the selected range.

ℹ️ *The **Font Color** can also be changed using the **Format Cells** dialog box, **Font** tab, **Color** box, but it takes longer.*

5. Highlight the range **A16:N16** and change the colour to **green**. Format the text in this range as **Bold** and click away from the range to see the effect.

ℹ️ *The last colour used will be shown on the **Font Color** button.*

6. As well as changing the colour of the text, the cell background can also be coloured. Highlight the range **A16:N16**.

7. Click the drop-down arrow on the **Fill Color** button, ⬛. Click on the lightest shade of **green** to add the background colour.

8. Fill cell **A1** with yellow and format the text as **Italic**. To copy the formatting from this cell, click **Format Painter**, ⬛.

9. Click on cell **A16** and notice how the format changes to match that in **A1**.

10. To make the range **B1:N1** look the same as **B16:N16**, select any cell in the range **B16:N16**, then click ⬛ and click and drag over **B1:N1**.

11. Close the workbook <u>without</u> saving.

Driving Lesson 73 - Rotate Text

▣ Park and Read

Text can be displayed vertically or at any angle within a cell.

⮑ Manoeuvres

1. Start a new workbook.

2. In cell **A2** enter **Candidate** and your full name into cell **B2**.

3. Click on cell **B2** and on the **Home** tab, click the **Orientation** button, 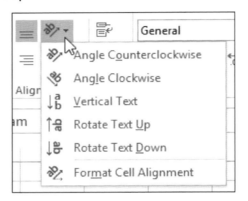, in the **Alignment** group.

4. Select **Vertical Text**. Your name is vertical and the row is increased in height automatically to hold the text.

ℹ️ *If the height of the row had been changed manually previously, then the row height will not change automatically. Adjust the row height manually.*

5. Click the **Undo** button, 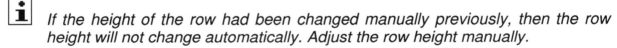, to return the text to normal.

6. Click the **Orientation** button, 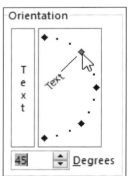. To display text at angles not listed, select the **Format Cell Alignment** option. Use the **Rotation** box on the right to drag the red diamond up to **45** degrees.

7. Click **OK**.

8. Change the orientation of the text in **B2** to **90** degrees.

9. Double click the column heading border between **B** and **C** to reduce the width of column to fit the entry. This could be used to create a candidate register or a form to log assignment results.

10. Close the workbook <u>without</u> saving.

Driving Lesson 74 - Freezing Panes

▣ Park and Read

Freeze Panes are used to keep specific rows and/or columns in view all the time. This is generally used for labels so that they stay on-screen while scrolling through a large worksheet. Placement of the active cell is important before freezing as all rows above, and all columns to the left, are frozen.

↷ Manoeuvres

1.   Open the workbook **Accounts**. This shows the cash flow for a small hotel.

2.   Before freezing the panes, one question: how much did the hotel pay in **October** for **Wages/NI** (National Insurance)?

3.   Scrolling to the right hides columns at the left and, scrolling down, rows from the top. These important rows/columns on the screen can be frozen. Press <**Ctrl Home**> to return to cell **A1**, then click in cell **B4** (the first cell containing data).

4.   Display the **View** tab and click **Freeze Panes** in the **Window** group. Select **Freeze Panes** from the menu. This freezes column **A** and rows **1** to **3**. Find **October's Wages**/**NI**, by scrolling down and across.

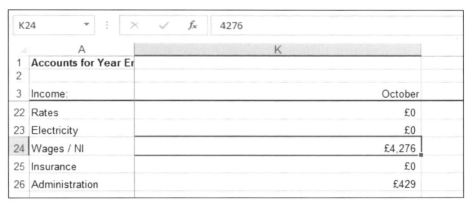

 If panes are frozen when a worksheet is saved, they will be still be frozen when the workbook is re-opened.

5.   When removing the frozen panes, the placing of the active cell is not important. Click the **Freeze Panes** button and then **Unfreeze Panes**.

6.   Click on cell **A4** and select to **Freeze Panes**. This freezes rows 1, 2 and 3 only. Scroll around the worksheet to see the effect.

7.   Remove the frozen panes with **Unfreeze Panes**.

8.   Select **Freeze Panes** and then choose **Freeze First Column**. This freezes column **A** only. Scroll around the worksheet to see the effect.

9.   Close the workbook <u>without</u> saving.

Driving Lesson 75 - Zoom

▣ Park and Read

Zoom is used to control the magnification of the worksheet window to see more by making the worksheet smaller, or to see less by making it bigger. The **Zoom** percentage is saved with the worksheet. **Zoom** is purely visual and does not affect the printing of the worksheet.

↱ Manoeuvres

1. Open the workbook **Shop**. This is a worksheet to show the profitability of a small market stall.

2. The **Zoom** slider is located at the right of the **Status Bar**. This is used by either dragging the slider left to decrease the zoom or right to increase it.

3. The buttons at either end can also be used to make bigger changes. Click and drag the slider to the left to display **80%**. The worksheet window is resized to **80%**.

4. Use ➕ to increase the percentage to **120%**.

5. Experiment with the **Zoom** slider.

6. There is a **Selection** option that fits a worksheet in the visible window. The required range must be selected first. Highlight the range **A1:N1** (the entire contents of the worksheet).

7. Display the **View** tab and, in the **Zoom** group, click the **Zoom to Selection** button. The zoom level fits the selection.

8. Click the **Zoom** button, 🔍 Zoom . The **Zoom** dialog box appears.

9. A specific magnification level can be selected here or a percentage entered into the **Custom** box.

10. Select **200%** below **Magnification** and click **OK**. Notice the effect.

11. Display the **Zoom** dialog box again and type **120** directly into the **Custom** box. Click **OK** and observe the effect.

12. Use the **Zoom to Selection** button to view all of the worksheet contents again.

13. Close the workbook <u>without</u> saving.

Driving Lesson 76 - Revision

▣ Park and Read

At the end of every section you get the chance to complete one or more revision exercises to develop your skills and prepare you for your ECDL certification test. You should aim to complete the following steps without referring back to the previous lessons.

↱ Manoeuvres

1.   Open the workbook **Balance Sheet**.

2.   The **Balance Sheet 2011** worksheet is displayed. To add a centred title, insert two rows at the top of the sheet.

3.   Add the title **Balance Sheet 2011** in **A1**. Change to font size of the title to **16pt** and the merge and centre from column **A** to **O**.

4.   Add **Freeze Panes** to keep **Rows 1** to **3** and **Columns A & B** on the screen permanently.

5.   Scroll to see the effect of the freeze.

6.   What was the **Shareholders Equity** for **Aug**?

7.   Remove the **Freeze Panes**.

8.   Using the zoom control display the information to fit within the screen.

9.   Change the **Zoom** back to **100%**.

10. Change the orientation of the page to **Landscape** and preview the worksheet.

11. Change the print options to fit the worksheet to one piece of paper.

12. Check the print preview to make sure it will print on one piece of paper. You can print the worksheet if you like.

13. Close the workbook <u>without</u> saving the changes.

 Sample answers can be found at the back of the guide.

Driving Lesson 77 - Revision

⌐ Manoeuvres

1. Open the workbook **Apples**.

2. Change the contents of cell **A1** to font size **16pt**.

3. Right align the labels at the top of the columns, including **Total**, i.e. the range **B3:E3**.

4. Change the **Zoom** percentage to **125**.

5. Change the display format for the numbers in the range **B8:E11** to currency with no decimal places and no symbol.

6. Change the width of **Column A** to **12.00** units

7. Widen columns **B** to **E** to **10.00** units.

8. Increase the row height of **Row 3** to **19.50** units.

9. Increase to height of rows **4** to **11** to **15.00** units.

10. Change the vertical alignment of the range **A3:E3** to the centre of the cells.

11. Insert a new column **D** to add **Grapes** to the worksheet. Add the title, **Grapes**. The numbers sold are 0, 1 and 5.

12. Complete the formula to total the new column in **D7**.

13. **Grapes** are bought at £8 and sold at £15. Add this data and the appropriate formulas to cell **D9** and **D11**. What is the **Total Profit** now?

14. Add border lines to the inside of the range **A3:F11** and a double line to the outside and remove the gridlines from the screen.

15. Change the colour of the labels in row **3** to **Blue**.

16. Change the background colour (**Fill Color** button) of the range **B4:F7** to a very pale orange.

17. Preview a copy of the worksheet. You can print it if you like.

18. Save the workbook as **Apples2** and close it.

i   *Sample answers can be found at the back of the guide.*

i   *Now complete the **Record of Achievement Matrix** at the back of the guide. You should only move on when confident with the topics and features described in this section.*

Section 9 Functions & Addressing

By the end of this section you should be able to:

Use the Functions Sum, Count and Average

Use the Functions Max, Min and IF

Use Relative and Absolute Addressing

Work through the **Driving Lessons** in this section to gain an understanding of the above features.

For each **Driving Lesson**, read all of the **Park and Read** instructions and then perform the numbered steps of the **Manoeuvres**. Complete the **Revision** exercise(s) at the end of the section to test your knowledge.

Driving Lesson 78 - Functions

◨ Park and Read

Functions are specialised formulas that make a calculation easier. Just as **Sum** totals a range of cells, other functions such as **Average**, **Min**, **Max** and **Count** can be used to simplify calculations.

Functions can be typed directly into a cell, e.g. **=SUM(A1:B6)**. The **Insert Function** button can also be used.

⌇ Manoeuvres

1. Open the workbook **Numbers**.

2. Click cell **B13** and type **=s**. A quick function list opens showing all functions starting with **s**. Scroll down the list and double click **SUM**.

3. Type the rest of the function **B3:B12)** and press <**Enter**> to complete the formula.

4. Click cell **D7**, then click the **Insert Function** button, ⌐*fx*⌐, on the **Formula Bar** to display the **Insert Function** dialog box.

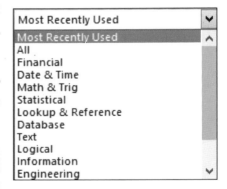

5. Click the drop-down box to the right of **Or select a category**. Click each function group to see all available functions.

6. Select the **Math & Trig** category and, from **Select a function**, scroll down the list and select **Sum**. An explanation of the function is given.

7. Click **OK** and a prompt for a range to be summed appears (it may already contain a guess as to the range required).

8. Click the **Collapse** button, ▦, at the right side of the **Number1** box. If this box hides the required range, drag clear of the numbers.

9. Click and drag to select the range **D3:D6**. Click the **Expand** button, ▦, in the box and the range appears.

10. Click **OK**. The function is entered into the worksheet and the result is displayed.

11. Close the worksheet <u>without</u> saving.

Driving Lesson 79 - Count

▣ Park and Read

The function **COUNT** counts the cells that contain numbers in a range.

COUNTA counts the number of cells that are <u>not</u> empty and **COUNTBLANK** counts empty cells.

↱ Manoeuvres

1. Open the workbook **Marks**. This shows the exam results for one student.

2. Click on cell **E7** and click the **Insert Function** button, f_x .

3. Select **Statistical** in the category list and then select **COUNT** in the **Select a function** list.

4. Click **OK** to display the **Function Arguments** box. Then click the **Collapse** button to the right of **Value1**.

5. Select the range **B4:B21** (the cells that might contain values).

6. **Expand** the **Function Arguments** dialog box and click **OK** to complete the function. **11** appears – the number of cells that contain numbers.

7. **Ali** failed to turn up for the German exam. Enter **0** in cell **B8**. The number of subjects now shows **12** as zero counts as a number.

8. **Ali** didn't sit the **Art** exam. Enter **NA** in cell **B18**. The number of subjects doesn't change as the value entered was not a number.

9. Delete the function in cell **E7**.

10. With **E7** still selected, click **Insert Function**, f_x , again and this time select **COUNTA** from **Statistical**. Click **OK**.

11. Select the range **B4:B21** and click **OK** (you do not need to collapse the **Function Arguments** dialog box if you do not want to). The number of subjects now appears as **16** as all cells with a value are now counted.

12. Delete the function in cell **E7**. Then insert the function **COUNTBLANK** from **Statistical**. Click **OK**, select the range **B4:B21** and click **OK**.

13. Notice how the number of blank cells has been counted (**2**). Delete the contents of **B9** and the result in **E7** increases (**3**).

14. Delete function in **E7** and replace it with the original **COUNT** function.

15. Leave the workbook open for the next lesson.

Driving Lesson 80 - Average & Round

▣ Park and Read

Average adds a list of numbers and divides by the count.

Sometimes it is required to show numerical data to a specific level of precision, for example to show a price field to the nearest pound or an age to the nearest year. To do this either use formatting (which does not change the actual content) or use the **Round** function.

↱ Manoeuvres

1. The workbook **Marks** should be open from the last exercise.

2. Click in cell **E8**. Click the **Insert Function** button, f_x.

3. Click on **Statistical** in the function category list and select **AVERAGE** in the **Select a function** list.

4. Click **OK** to display the **Function Arguments** box for **AVERAGE**.

5. Select the range **B4:B21** (you can move the **Function Arguments** box to do this or collapse it). Click **OK** to complete the function. The result is **63**.

6. The **0** for **German** is reducing the average. It is decided that **Ali** should not have been registered for **German**, so delete the zero in cell **B8**. Note the increase in **Average** mark – it has increased to **69**.

7. With the workbook **Marks** open, start a new workbook. In cell **B3** enter **27.32** and in cell **B4** enter **27.68**.

8. Highlight **B3:B4** and format the range as **Number** with **0** decimal places. The numbers are displayed to the nearest whole number. The cell content has not been changed, only the appearance. **B4** displays **28** in the cell. Click on **B4**. The **Formula Bar** still shows the cell content as **27.68**.

9. In **C3** enter the formula **=B3*1.15** to calculate the new value for **B3** after a 15% increase. Copy the formula down to **C4**.

10. In **D3** enter the formula **=ROUND(C3,0)**. This rounds the value in **C3** to have **0** decimal places. Copy the formula down to **D4**. The values are shown as whole numbers.

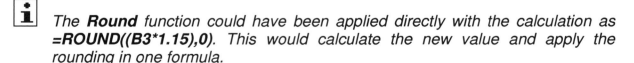

ℹ️ *The **Round** function could have been applied directly with the calculation as* ***=ROUND((B3*1.15),0)***. *This would calculate the new value and apply the rounding in one formula.*

11. Close the workbook <u>without</u> saving, but leave the workbook **Marks** open.

Driving Lesson 81 - Maximum and Minimum

🅿 Park and Read

MAX the function for maximum. Finds and displays the largest number in a selected range.

MIN the function for minimum. Finds and displays the smallest number in a selected range.

☞ Manoeuvres

1. The workbook **Marks** should still be open. If not, open it.

2. Enter the text **Highest Mark** in cell **D9** and **Lowest Mark** in cell **D10**.

3. Click in cell **E9**. Click the **Insert Function** button, f_x.

4. Click on **Statistical** in the function category list and select **MAX** in the **Select a function** list.

5. Click **OK** to display the **Function Arguments** box.

6. Select the same range as before: **B4:B21**.

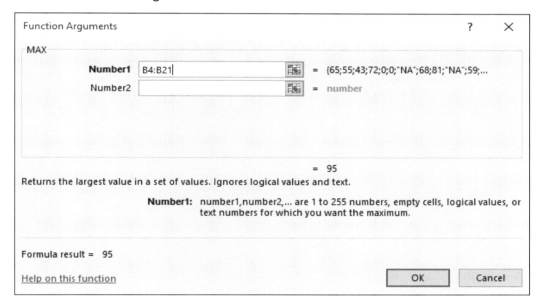

7. Click **OK** to complete the function. The highest mark is **95**.

8. In cell **E10** enter the **MIN** function using the same range to display the lowest mark.

9. To test the four functions created, change the marks in **B17** to **50** and **B6** to **83** and note the changes in the function values.

10. Save the workbook as **Marks2** and then close it.

Driving Lesson 82 - IF

⊞ Park and Read

The logical function **IF** compares the contents of a cell and, if a logical test is met, performs one action; if not, it performs another.

=IF(Logical_test,Value_if_true,Value_if_false)

For instance, if the value in cell **A1** is greater than 10 then multiply it by 3, if not, multiply it by 2. This is expressed as: **=IF(A1>10,A1*3,A1*2)**

The **IF** function is sometimes described as **IF THEN ELSE**. **IF** the condition is true **THEN** do this **ELSE** do that. The function parts are separated by commas.

↱ Manoeuvres

1. On a blank worksheet, enter the labels **Interest Calculation** in **B1**, **Balance** in cell **B3** and **Interest** in cell **B4**.

2. Enter **200** in **C3** for your bank balance.

3. The interest on your money depends on whether the balance is over or under **£100**. Click in cell **C4** and as an alternative to using the **Insert Function** button, display the **Formulas** tab and click **Logical** in the **Function Library**. Select **IF** from the list.

4. The **Function Arguments** dialog box appears. Complete the function as shown below.

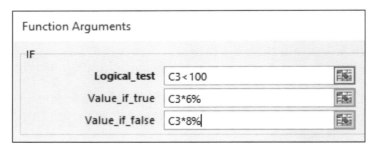

5. Click **OK** to complete the function. The function looks at the value of cell **C3** and, if it is less than **100**, calculates the interest at **6%** of the value, otherwise it calculates it at **8%**.

6. The result of the function, the interest, depends on the balance. Move to **C3** and enter **1000**. The interest is **£80**, the higher rate (8%).

7. Enter **50** into **C3** and the interest is **£3** (6%).

8. Experiment by changing the balance and watching the interest change. The **IF** function is very powerful.

9. Close the workbook <u>without</u> saving.

Driving Lesson 83 - Relative Addressing

▣ Park and Read

As a formula is copied to a new location, by default the cell references in the formula change automatically. The new calculation is performed on cells in the same positions relative to the original formula, e.g. references to **B2+B3** become **C2+C3** then **D2+D3**, as the formula is copied to the right from column to column. This is **Relative Addressing**.

⤵ Manoeuvres

1. Start a new workbook.

2. In **B2** enter **7** and **B3** enter **8**.

3. Select cell **B4** and click the **AutoSum** button on the **Formulas** tab to add the contents of the two cells above. Press <**Enter**> to accept the range and perform the calculation.

4. Select cell **B4**. The answer should be **15** and the formula **=SUM(B2:B3)**.

5. Use the **Fill Handle** to copy this formula across to cell **C4**. The displayed answer is **0** because the two cells above are empty. Click on cell **C4** to display the formula in the **Formula Bar**, **=SUM(C2:C3)**. It sums the two cells directly above which are empty.

6. Enter **3** in cell **C2** and **5** in cell **C3**. The answer in cell **C4** is now **8**.

7. Copy cell **B4** to cell **E8**. What is the formula in cell **E8**?

8. Enter any two numbers in the cells **E6** and **E7** to test the formula.

9. Close the workbook <u>without</u> saving.

10. Open the workbook **Accounts**. This is the basic cash flow (the flow of money in and out) for a small hotel.

11. Click on cell **B14**. This sums the cash coming into the hotel for **January**.

12. Use any method to copy this formula to the range **C14:N14**.

13. Click on cell **E14** (the turnover for **April**). It sums the same range of rows as in cell **B14**, except using the cells in column **E**.

14. Close the workbook <u>without</u> saving.

ℹ *Sample answers can be found at the back of the guide.*

Driving Lesson 84 - Absolute Addressing

▣ Park and Read

If you want to keep a cell reference the same when copying you need to use **Absolute Addressing**. When formulas use the same cell, it is easy to make changes to all the formulas.

An **Absolute** reference uses the **$** sign. For example, **D7** is a **Relative** address that will change if the formula is copied and **$D$7** is an **Absolute** address that will stay the same. The dollar signs fix the cell so that it can be copied without changing.

↱ Manoeuvres

1.   Open the workbook **Absolute**.

2.   The average mark is calculated in cell **B23** as **63**. Click in cell **B23** and view the formula (the **Average** function).

3.   To compare each mark with the average, click in cell **C4** and enter the formula **=B4-B23**. The answer is **2** (65 is 2 marks above the average of 63).

4.   Use the **Fill Handle** to copy the formula in cell **C4** down to cell **C21**. Something has gone wrong – can you tell what?

5.   The formula in **C4** contained relative cell addresses and so *Excel* automatically updated them when they were copied. Click cell **C5** and notice the formula is **=B5-B24**. **B24** is empty, therefore the answer is **55**.

6.   Click in cell **C4**. The cell reference **B23** needs to be fixed, i.e. made **Absolute**. Change the formula to **=B4-$B$23**.

7.   Use the **Fill Handle** to copy cell **C4** down to **C21** again. The average mark **63** in **B23** is now used in all the formulas in column **C**.

8.   Change the **English Literature** mark to **70**. All the cells in the range **C4:C21** change because **B23** has changed.

9.   Close the workbook without saving.

10. Open the workbook **World Population**. This workbook contains some population statistics.

11. The population of Europe in 1975 was **424** million. The world population was **1953** million. Click on cell **C8**, Europe's population as a percentage of the world. Note the formula **=B8/$B$11**. The cell **B11** has been made **Absolute** and does not change in the formulas in column **C**.

12. Close the workbook without saving.

Driving Lesson 85 - Revision

▣ Park and Read

At the end of every section you get the chance to complete one or more revision exercises to develop your skills and prepare you for your ECDL certification test. You should aim to complete the following steps without referring back to the previous lessons.

↱ Manoeuvres

1. What name is given to cell references in a formula which change when the formula is copied to a new location?

2. What symbol is used to show that references are **Absolute**?

3. If a formula in a cell is **=C2+$E$5** what would the formula be if this was copied   a) down one cell? b) to the right one cell?

4. If you copied the formula **=B3+D4** in **C6** to cell **F8**, what would the formula be in cell **F8**? You can create this on a worksheet if it helps.

5. When would you use **Absolute Addressing**?

6. Start a new workbook and create the worksheet below.

▲	A	B	C	D	E
1					
2					
3		Number Sold		20	
4		Buying Price		5	
5		Selling Price		6	
6		Profit			
7					

7. The reason for using column **D** for the numbers is that the text is too long for column **B**. It spilled over into column **C**. Widen column **B**.

8. Delete column **C**.

9. Calculate the **Profit** in **C6** (remember to use brackets).

10. Change the **Number Sold** to **534**, the **Buying Price** to **2.56** and the **Selling Price** to **3.99**.

11. Format cell **C6** to display currency with two decimal places.

12. How much is the **Profit**?

13. Close the workbook <u>without</u> saving.

ℹ *Sample answers can be found at the back of the guide.*

Driving Lesson 86 - Revision

Manoeuvres

1. The following data represents sales figures for a group of salespersons. Construct the spreadsheet and add the data at the positions shown.

	A	B	C	D
1	Analysis of Sales Figures			
2				
3	Salesperson	Sales	Average*/-	
4	Smith	1300		
5	Brown	8965		
6	Bloggs	21050		
7	White	17800		
8	Green			
9	Chapman	670		
10	Hall	1809		
11				
12	Total			
13	Average Sales			
14	No of Salespersons			
15	Lowest Sales			
16	Highest Sales			

2. Enter the functions for **Total** and **Average Sales** in **B12** and **B13**.

3. The number of salespersons is calculated using the **COUNT** function (Remember to count the sales figures, not the salespersons' names).

4. Complete the high and low sales use **MAX** and **MIN**.

5. The **Average +/-** column is to be the variation of an individual's sales compared to the average, calculated by subtracting the average sales value from the individual's sales. For **C4** this is **=B4-B13** (Remember **Absolute** and **Relative** addressing if copying formulas down the column).

6. What is the result in cell **C10**?

7. Save the workbook as **Sales** then close it.

ℹ️ *It is very important to decide whether to put a zero in cell **B8** or to leave it blank. Try it! The answers will be different.*

ℹ️ *Now complete the **Record of Achievement Matrix** at the back of the guide. You should only move on when confident with the topics and features described in this section.*

Section 10 Charts

By the end of this section you should be able to:

Create a Chart

Select Chart Type

Move, Copy and Resize Charts

Format a Chart

Print a Chart

Use Chart Options

Work through the **Driving Lessons** in this section to gain an understanding of the above features.

For each **Driving Lesson**, read all of the **Park and Read** instructions and then perform the numbered steps of the **Manoeuvres**. Complete the **Revision** exercise(s) at the end of the section to test your knowledge.

Driving Lesson 87 - Introducing Charts

▣ Park and Read

Charts are used to show numerical information in a graphical way that is clear and easy to understand. There are many chart styles available in *Excel*, but the following list includes the four most popular types:

Column - Shaded vertical columns

Bar - Shaded horizontal bars

Line - Points connected by a line

Pie - Data as slices of a circular pie

There are also various 3-D charts and different versions of the same chart type.

i *Charts can appear on the same worksheet as the data (known as an* ***embedded*** *chart) or on its own sheet.*

⌐ Manoeuvres

1. Open the workbook **Charts**. This contains both an embedded chart and charts created on separate sheets.

2. Take a look at the **Data** worksheet. This sheet contains the source information used for the charts. Scroll down the worksheet to see an embedded chart under the data.

3. Display the **London Rainfall** sheet. This is a chart that has been created on a separate sheet.

4. Display the **Mumbai Rainfall** and **London v Adelaide** sheets. These charts are similar to the **London Rainfall** chart and appear on separate sheets.

5. Close the workbook **Charts** <u>without</u> saving.

Driving Lesson 88 - Creating Charts

▣ Park and Read

Charts are usually placed on the same worksheet as the data they are based on. This is called an **Embedded Chart**. Embedded charts can be moved, resized and deleted.

↱ Manoeuvres

1.   Open the workbook **Rainfall**. This contains the average rainfall for four major cities in the world. Charts are to be created to show this information.

2.   To chart **London's** rainfall as a column chart, select the range **A1:B13** (this is the rainfall values and the labels).

3.   Display the **Insert** tab and click **Insert Column or Bar Chart** in the **Charts** group.

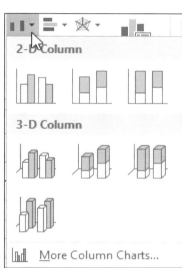

4.   The **Column** chart options are displayed. Under **2-D Column** select the first option, **Clustered Column**. The chart is created and placed on the **Rainfall** sheet.

5.   The chart is active and the **Ribbon** displays a new group of tabs under the banner **Chart Tools**. The **Design** tab is selected.

6.   The chart can be moved by clicking and dragging. Place the cursor on the chart border (it displays a four-headed arrow). Click and drag it to the left and below the data.

7.   To resize the chart, click and drag on any of the handles around it, ○ (any corner or the centre of any side). Dragging inwards will make the chart smaller, outwards will make it bigger. Try it!

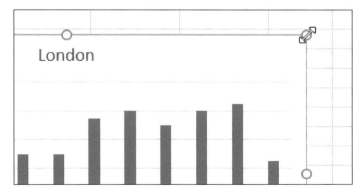

ℹ️   *To delete an embedded chart, simply click on it to select it and press <**Delete**>.*

8.   Save the workbook as **Rainfall2** and leave it open.

Driving Lesson 89 - Moving Charts Between Worksheets

⃞ Park and Read

Charts can be moved and placed on a separate worksheet.

⟲ Manoeuvres

1. The workbook **Rainfall2** should still be open. A column chart of the rainfall in **Mumbai** is now going to be created.

2. Two separate ranges need to be selected to chart **Mumbai's** rainfall, the labels and the actual rainfall data. Select **A1:A13**.

3. Hold <**Ctrl**> down while selecting the other range **C1:C13**. Two ranges should be selected.

	A	B	C	D	E	F
1	RAINFALL(cms)	London	Mumbai	Adelaide	Tokyo	
2	Jan	5.5	0.5	1.8	5.0	
3	Feb	4.0	0.5	1.8	7.0	
4	Mar	3.8	0.0	2.5	10.0	
5	Apr	3.9	0.0	4.0	14.0	
6	May	4.5	2.0	7.0	13.0	
7	Jun	4.5	24.0	8.0	18.0	
8	Jul	5.8	24.0	7.0	14.0	
9	Aug	6.0	24.0	6.0	14.0	
10	Sep	5.5	24.0	5.0	21.0	
11	Oct	6.0	4.5	4.5	22.0	
12	Nov	6.3	1.0	3.0	10.0	
13	Dec	4.3	0.0	2.5	6.0	
14						

4. Display the **Insert** tab and click the **Insert Column or Bar Chart** button in the **Charts** group.

5. The **Column** chart options are displayed as before. Select the same option, a **Clustered Column**. The chart is embedded and placed on the **Rainfall** sheet with the data, overlapping the data and the previous chart.

6. Drag the chart to the right so that it doesn't overlap the data or the other embedded chart.

7. To place the chart on a separate worksheet, click the **Move Chart** button on the **Design** tab. The **Move Chart** dialog box is displayed.

8. Select the **New sheet** option and enter the sheet name **Mumbai Rainfall** as a replacement for **Chart1**.

9. Click **OK** to move the chart. It now appears on its own sheet.

10. Save the workbook using the same name **Rainfall2** and close it.

Driving Lesson 90 - Chart Types

 Park and Read

Different types of chart are used for different types of data. The most common type of chart is a **Column** chart (as seen already). It displays the data in columns and is used to compare values.

Bar charts are column charts where the values are horizontal bars and not vertical columns.

Line charts are used to display the change of values over time.

Pie charts display values as slices of a circle. The size of each slice represents the value of the data on which it is based, as a fraction of the total. Pie charts are used to show values as a part of the whole.

Manoeuvres

1. Open the workbook **Computer Data**. Four different types of chart are to be created using the same data.

2. Highlight the data in the cells **A3:B8** (include the titles but not the totals, as they are rarely included in charts).

3. Display the **Insert** tab and, from the **Charts** group, click **Insert Pie or Doughnut Chart**, ⏺. Select the first option: a basic **Pie**.

4. The *chart title*, **Sales**, is added automatically. Move the chart to a separate worksheet named **Pie Chart**.

5. Return to the **Data** sheet and, with the same range selected, use the **Insert Column or Bar Chart** button, ▮▮, to create a basic **Clustered Column** chart on a new sheet named **Column Chart**.

6. Next, return to the **Data** sheet and, using the **Insert Column or Bar Chart** button again, create a **Clustered Bar** chart on its own **Bar Chart** sheet.

7. Finally, return to the **Data** sheet and, using the **Insert Line or Area Chart** button, ⩗⩗, create a simple **Line** chart on its own **Line Chart** sheet.

8. The sheet tabs should appear as shown below.

 You can change the type of chart once you have created it. You will see how to do this later.

9. Save the workbook as **Computer Data2** and leave it open for the next lesson.

Driving Lesson 91 - Copy, Move & Resize Charts

▣ Park and Read

Charts can be copied, resized and deleted.

↱ Manoeuvres

1. Charts can be copied from one sheet to another. Using the workbook opened in the previous lesson, display the **Bar Chart** sheet tab.

2. Click the chart to select it (if it is not already).

3. Display the **Home** tab and click the **Copy** button, in the **Clipboard** group (or press <**Ctrl C**>).

4. To copy the chart to the **Data** sheet, display it, select cell **A11** and then click the **Paste** button (or press <**Ctrl V**>) to paste the chart onto the **Data** sheet. Paste

5. The chart is too big. Resize and reposition it so that both the chart and the data fits on the screen.

6. Charts can be copied from workbook to workbook. Display the **Line Chart** sheet and copy the chart.

7. Start a new workbook. Paste the chart onto **Sheet1** and it appears embedded.

8. Display the **Design** tab, click **Move Chart**, and move the chart to a new sheet named **Line Chart**. Click **OK** and it now appears on its own sheet.

ⓘ *Charts can be moved using standard* ***Cut*** *(<Ctrl X>) and* ***Paste*** *(<Ctrl V>) commands.*

9. Close the new workbook <u>without</u> saving.

10. Display the **Data** sheet of the **Computer Data2** workbook.

11. Click the embedded bar chart on the **Data** sheet to select it and then click **Copy**. Place the active cell beneath the chart and click **Paste** to create an identical duplicate.

ⓘ *To select a chart, try clicking its border rather than the elements inside.*

12. To delete the copied chart, select it and then press <**Delete**>.

13. Save the workbook as **Computer Data2** and leave it open.

Driving Lesson 92 - Formatting Charts

🅿 Park and Read

All parts of a chart including the title, colours, axes, text, gridlines and plot area can be changed.

🔁 Manoeuvres

1. The workbook **Computer Data2** should still be open. Select the **Bar Chart** sheet tab and place the mouse pointer over different parts of the chart (without clicking). Read the **ToolTips** that appear.

2. Any and every part of a chart can be changed by formatting. Click the **Chart Title** (**Sales**) to select it. Then, display the **Home** tab and use the options in the **Font** group to change the font to **Arial**, size **20**, colour red.

3. Click the chart title's text again to place the cursor. You can now edit the text – change the title to **Computer Sales 2015**.

4. You don't want the chart title. On the **Design** tab, click the **Add Chart Element** button, click **Chart Title**, and select **None**.

ℹ️ *You can also select chart elements and press <**Delete**> to remove them.*

5. Point at the white background behind the bars (the **Plot Area**) and click. Display the **Format** tab and click **Shape Fill** in the **Shape Styles** group.

ℹ️ *The **Picture**, **Gradient** and **Texture** options can be used to add a picture, gradient colour or simple texture effect to a background.*

6. Select a light orange colour and observe the effect.

ℹ️ *The colour of the chart background is more important if viewed on screen. Printed charts can be left as the default (no fill colour) to save ink.*

7. Click the **Column Chart** sheet to make it active.

8. To change the colour of the columns, point at any column and then click to select them all. Change the colour to **Red** using the **Shape Fill** button.

9. The colour of a single data point can also be changed. With all columns currently selected, click the **Sunderland** column. Only that data point is now selected.

10. Select **Blue** using the **Shape Fill** button.

11. Display the **Pie Chart** sheet and change the colour of the **Sunderland** slice <u>only</u> to yellow.

12. Save the workbook using the same name and leave it open.

Driving Lesson 93 - Chart Options

▣ Park and Read

All parts of a chart, including the titles, legend, data labels and axis text can be changed. Text boxes can also be added to include supporting information.

⤴ Manoeuvres

1. **Computer Data2** should be open with the pie chart selected. Click on an empty part of the chart, away from the pie chart graphic, to deselect it.

2. *Data labels* can be displayed which show the values used to create the chart. Display the **Design** tab and click **Add Chart Element**.

3. Click **Data Labels** and a submenu appears. Without clicking, place your mouse pointer over each option (e.g. **Center**, **Inside End**, **Outside End**) and notice the effect on the chart.

4. Finally, select **Outside End** to apply this setting.

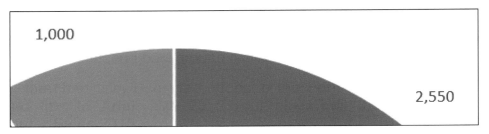

ℹ️ *The **CHART ELEMENTS** button,* ➕ *, can also be used to add or remove various chart elements.*

5. Data labels can be shown as values or percentages. Click the **Add Chart Element** button, select **Data Labels** and then **More Data Label Options**.

6. The **Format Data Labels** task pane appears. Make sure **Value** and **Percentage** are both selected and notice the effect on the chart.

7. Remove the tick in **Value** and only percentages are shown on the chart.

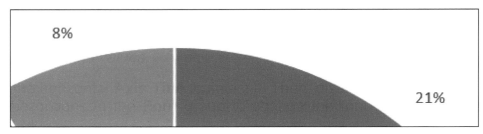

Driving Lesson 93 - Continued

8. Use the **Add Chart Element** button to set **Data Labels** to **None**. This removes the data labels.

9. Next, click the **Add Chart Element** button again and select **Legend**. Without clicking, place your mouse pointer over each option (e.g. **Right**, **Top**, **Left**, **Bottom**) and notice the effect on the chart.

10. Finally, select **Right** to apply this setting.

■ Newcastle

Sunderland

■ Swindon

■ Cambridge

■ Edinburgh

11. Click the legend to select it. Then, display the **Home** tab and use the options in the **Font** group to change the font to **Arial**, size **14**, colour blue.

12. With the legend still selected, click the **Fill Color** button, , and select a pale green. The legend background is filled with colour.

13. Select the chart title. Use the buttons in the **Font** group to change the **Legend** text to **Arial**, size **20**, colour blue. Edit the **Chart Title** to **Computer Sales 2015**.

Computer Sales 2015

 *You can also access formatting settings by right clicking a chart element and selecting **Format Chart Title**, **Format Plot Area**, **Format Legend**, etc.*

14. Display the **Column Chart** sheet. On the **Design** tab, click **Add Chart Element**, select **Axis Titles** and click **Primary Horizontal**. Notice the **Axis Title** box.

Swindon

Axis Title

15. Use the **Add Chart Element** button to apply a **Primary Vertical** axis title.

 Many chart types have horizontal (bottom) and vertical (left) axis bars which show chart scales and values.

16. Click the horizontal **Axis Title** to select it. Then, display the **Home** tab and use the options in the **Font** group to change the font to **Arial**, size **14**, colour blue.

Driving Lesson 93 - Continued

17. Repeat the same change to the left, vertical **Axis Title**.

18. Once created, chart types can be easily changed. Display the **Bar Chart** sheet and select the chart.

19. Click the **Change Chart Type** button on the **Design** tab. The **Change Chart Type** dialog box appears.

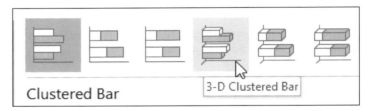

20. With the **All Charts** tab selected, click each of the chart types on the left to see a preview of the charts available. You can select from any of these.

21. Select **Pie** and click **OK**. The bar chart is converted into a pie chart.

22. Click the **Change Chart Type** button again and select **Bar**. From the types of bar chart available, select **3-D Clustered Bar**.

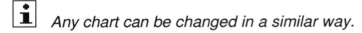

23. Variants of this chart type are shown below as previews. The default variant is fine, so click **OK**. Notice the impressive effect.

i *Any chart can be changed in a similar way.*

24. Make the **Line Chart** sheet active. To format the line, click on it to select it. Display the **FORMAT** tab and click the **Shape Outline** button. From the menu select **Red** from the **Standard Colors** section.

25. Click the **Shape Outline** button again, click **Weight** and then select **3pt** as the thickness. The line is now red and thicker.

i *Excel features a number of impressive chart styles to simplify the formatting process.*

26. With the line chart still selected, display the **Design** tab and take a look at the **Chart Styles** group.

27. Try selecting some of the styles to see them applied to the selected chart. Some of these styles are very impressive.

28. Save the workbook using the same name and close it.

Driving Lesson 94 - Printing Charts

Park and Read

Embedded charts are printed as part of a worksheet via the standard **File** and **Print** options. You can also choose to print only a chart.

Manoeuvres

1.   Open the workbook **Rainfall2** created earlier.

2.   Display the **Mumbai Rainfall** sheet (if it is not already open).

3.   Click the **File** tab and select **Print** (or press <**Ctrl P**>). Notice the print preview – this is how the chart will look when printed.

4.   Return to the worksheet without printing and display **Sheet1**. This sheet contains both data and a chart.

5.   Click the **File** tab and select **Print**. Notice the print preview – this is how the chart will look when printed; both the data and chart appear.

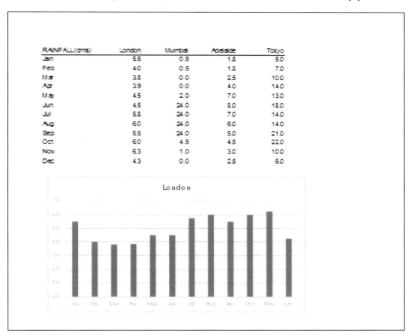

6.   Return to the worksheet without printing and select the chart.

7.   Click the **File** tab and select **Print**. Notice that only the selected chart will now be printed.

8.   Print a copy of the selected chart (or return to the worksheet without printing).

9.   Close the workbook without saving.

Driving Lesson 95 - Revision

▣ Park and Read

At the end of every section you get the chance to complete one or more revision exercises to develop your skills and prepare you for your ECDL certification test. You should aim to complete the following steps without referring back to the previous lessons.

⌒ Manoeuvres

1. What tab is used to create a chart in *Excel*?

2. Name three commonly used types of chart.

3. If you were given the weekly sales figures for a company, what type of chart would you create to best demonstrate the data?

4. What type of chart would you create to represent the breakdown of costs involved with producing a particular product?

5. A **Bar Chart** and a **Column Chart** are similar, but what is the difference?

ℹ️ *Sample answers can be found at the back of the guide.*

Driving Lesson 96 - Revision

⌐ Manoeuvres

1. Open the workbook **Analysis**.

2. Create a 2D pie chart using the range **A3:B10**.

3. Move the chart to a new worksheet called **Sales Chart**.

4. Change the chart title to **Sales Analysis Figures**.

5. Add **Data Labels** to show **Value** as **Outside End**.

6. Change the **Legend** so it appears at the top of the chart (under the title).

7. Format the title to be **16** point and **Blue** text.

8. Remove the **Legend** and print a copy of the pie chart.

9. The chart should appear as below.

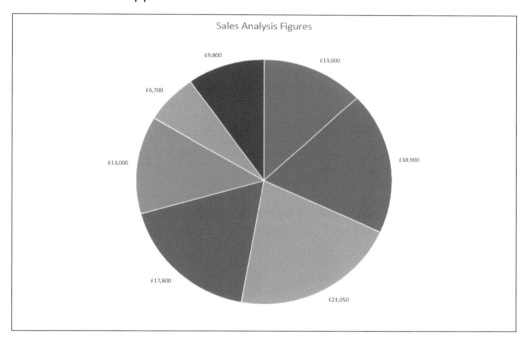

10. Change the chart to a **Clustered Bar Chart**.

11. Add appropriate horizontal and vertical axis labels.

12. Save the workbook as **Analysis2** and close it.

13. Close *Excel*.

*Now complete the **Record of Achievement Matrix** at the back of the guide. You should only move on when confident with the topics and features described in this section.*

Answers

Driving Lesson 10

    2.   By a heavy border and the cell reference is displayed in the Formula Bar

    3.   There is only 1 by default - Sheet1. More can be added

    4.   a) Increase Font Size

            b) Merge & Center

            c) Format Painter

            d) Fill Color

    5.   There are 6 groups displayed on the Data group

    6.   The other group is called Calculation

    7.   Close

Driving Lesson 11

    2.   The key press <Alt F4> closes the application

    3.   Three buttons; Save, Undo and Redo

    4.   <End →>

    5.   1048576

    6.   <Ctrl Home>

Driving Lesson 15

    7.   The workbook Budget is active as it has just been opened.

Driving Lesson 30

    2.   Column

    3.   42

    4.   21

    7.   37

Driving Lesson 49

    4.   £208

    7.   £170

    9.   £80

Driving Lesson 50

    4.   **Wednesday** and 2012 was a leap year

    10.   23725 days old at age 65 (approximately).

Driving Lesson 76

6.   £9876

Driving Lesson 77

13.   £388

Driving Lesson 83

6.   =SUM(E6:E7)

Driving Lesson 85

1.   Relative Addressing

2. $

3.   a) =C3+$E$5   b) =D2+$E$5

4.   =E5+G6

5.   When one cell contains information to be used by formulas in several locations.

12.   £763.62

Driving Lesson 86

6.   -6790

Driving Lesson 95

1.   Insert

2.   Column, Bar, Line and Pie are popular charts.

3.   Line or Column chart

4.   Pie chart

5.   In a column chart the data is represented by vertical columns. In a Bar chart data is displayed using horizontal bars. The two axes change places.

Record of Achievement Matrix

The **Record of Achievement** matrix can be used to measure progress through this guide. This is a learning reinforcement process – you judge when you are competent.

Three tick boxes are provided for each exercise. Column 1 should be ticked for **no knowledge** of the subject or topic covered, 2 for **some knowledge**, and 3 for **competent**. A section is only complete when you have ticked column 3 for all exercises.

Tick the Relevant Boxes   **1**: No Knowledge   **2**: Some Knowledge   **3**: Competent

Section	No.	Driving Lesson	1	2	3
1 Getting Started	1	Starting Excel			
	2	The Excel Screen			
	3	The Ribbon			
	4	Quick Access Toolbar			
	5	The Worksheet Window			
	6	Moving Around			
	7	Help			
	8	Preferences			
	9	Closing Excel			
2 Open and Close Workbooks	12	Opening a Workbook			
	13	Closing a Workbook			
	14	Using Scroll Bars			
	15	Opening Multiple Workbooks			
3 Creating & Saving Workbooks	17	Starting a New Workbook			
	18	Entering Labels			
	19	Entering Numbers			
	20	Saving a New Workbook			
	21	Saving a Named Workbook			
	22	Saving in Different Formats			
	23	Saving as a Template			
4 Formulas	26	Formulas			
	27	Brackets			
	28	AutoSum			
	29	Checking for Errors			
5 Workbooks	32	Multiple Worksheets			
	33	Switch Between Open Workbooks			
	34	Renaming Sheets			
	35	Copying and Moving Sheets			
	36	Inserting and Deleting Sheets			

Tick the Relevant Boxes   **1**: No Knowledge   **2**: Some Knowledge   **3**: Competent

Section	No.	Driving Lesson	1	2	3
6 Editing	38	Editing Cells			
	39	Delete Cell Contents			
	40	Using Undo and Redo			
	41	Ranges			
	42	Using the Fill Handle			
	43	Copying Cells			
	44	Moving Cells			
	45	Copying & Moving Between Workbooks			
	46	Finding Specific Text			
	47	Replacing Text			
	48	Sorting			
7 Printing	51	Printing			
	52	Print Preview			
	53	Page Setup			
	54	Margins			
	55	Printing a Selection			
	56	Headers and Footers			
	57	Print Titles			
	58	Displaying and Printing Formulas			
8 Formatting	61	Formatting			
	62	Bold, Italic & Underline			
	63	Font & Font Size			
	64	Format Number			
	65	Dates			
	66	Alignment			
	67	Changing Column Width			
	68	Changing Row Height			
	69	Inserting Rows and Columns			
	70	Deleting Rows and Columns			
	71	Adding Borders			
	72	Adding Colour			
	73	Rotating Text			
	74	Freezing Panes			
	75	Zoom			

Tick the Relevant Boxes   **1**: No Knowledge   **2**: Some Knowledge   **3**: Competent

Section	**No.**	**Driving Lesson**	1	2	3
9 Functions & Addressing	78	Functions			
	79	Count			
	80	Average and Round			
	81	Maximum and Minimum			
	82	IF			
	83	Relative Addressing			
	84	Absolute Addressing			
10 Charts	87	Introducing Charts			
	88	Creating Charts			
	89	Moving Charts			
	90	Chart Types			
	91	Copy, Move and Resize Charts			
	92	Formatting Charts			
	93	Chart Options			
	94	Printing Charts			

Glossary

Addressing	A method of referencing cells, relative or absolute
Alignment	The position of data in a cell
AutoSum	A function to sum a range of numbers
Average	Function that adds a range and divides the number of numbers
Border	The edge of a cell, type and colour of line
Chart	A pictorial representation of data
Count	Function that displays the number of numbers in a range
Embedded Chart	A chart placed on a standard worksheet, usually with the source data
Excel	Spreadsheet application (app)
Excel Options	Customisation of basic options
Fill Handle	A cursor used to copy data
Font	A type or style of text
Footer	Information appearing on the bottom of every printed page
Format	Changing the appearance of information
Formula	A calculation, can use values and/or cell references
Freeze Panes	Fixing information on screen so that it is not affected by scrolling
Function	Specialised formulas that make calculations easier
Header	Information appearing on the top of every printed page
HTML	A format that can be read over the Internet (**H**yper**T**ext **M**arkup **L**anguage)
IF	Logical function that a carries out a test and performs one action if true and another if false
Maximum	Function that displays the largest number in a range
Minimum	Function that displays the smallest number in a range
Pixel	Small squares that make up the screen, normally 1024 by 768
Range	A group of adjacent cells
Workbook	A spreadsheet file
Worksheet	A single page within a workbook
Zoom	Worksheet magnification on-screen only

Index